"YOUR FRIENDLY NEIGHBOR"

"YOUR FRIENDLY NEIGHBOR"

THE STORY OF GEORGIA'S COCA-COLA BOTTLING FAMILIES

by Mike Cheatham

in association with

the Atlanta History Center

Mercer University Press
1979   1999
Twenty Years of Publishing Excellence

ISBN 0-86554-686-X / MUP / H506

Published by
Mercer University Press
6316 Peake Road
Macon, Georgia 31210-3960

The author and publisher express their appreciation to The Coca-Cola Company for permission to include excerpts from *The Coca-Cola Company: An Illustrated Profile of a Worldwide Company* (Atlanta: The Coca-Cola Company, 1974), specifically part three, "The Early Bottlers." Coke and Coca-Cola are registered trademarks of The Coca-Cola Company.

Portions of this book originally appeared in Mike Cheatham, "'They're Thirsty on Main Street and All Over': Georgia's Coca-Cola Bottlers as Entrepreneurs and Civic Leaders," *Georgia Historical Quarterly*, vol. LXXX, no. 1, Spring 1996, 117-135.

This book was made possible by a grant from The Community Foundation for Greater Atlanta, Inc.

∞The paper used in this publication meets the minimum requirements of American National Standard for Information Sciences — Permanence of Paper for Printed Library Materials, ANSI Z39.48-1984.

Library of Congress Cataloging-in-Publication Data
Cheatham, Mike
"Your friendly neighbor": the story of Georgia's Coca-Cola bottling families/by Mike Cheatham. — 1st edition
p. cm.
    Includes bibliographical references and index.
    ISBN 0-86554-686-X (alk. paper).
    1. Coca-Cola Company — History. 2. Soft drink industry — Georgia — History.
3. Soft drink industry — United States — History.
I. Title.
HD9349.S634C627   1999
    338.7'66362'0973 — dc21   99-36854
                                                                                              CIP

CONTENTS

This book is dedicated to the memory of Mr. Willie Barron (1898–1977), "your friendly neighbor who bottles Coca-Cola." That was his contribution. His legacy is that and so much more, in terms of what he brought to the many lives he touched in his territory and elsewhere.

Mike Cheatham
Athens, Georgia, 1998

1

A CENTURY OF LEADERS

At the turn of the twentieth century, dozens of Georgians tied their fortunes to the bottling of a simple carbonated beverage—Coca-Cola. Capitalizing on the popularity of this fountain treat, these entrepreneurs signed contracts in perpetuity with The Coca-Cola Company of Atlanta, granting them the right to produce and package the product. This dedicated and influential body of bottlers not only brought the beverage "within an arm's length of desire" for Georgians, but associated the Coca-Cola business with Main Streets all over the state. In addition to material rewards, these bottlers earned the respect of their neighbors in ways seldom duplicated by their corporate cousins with the syrup-purveying parent firm.[1]

In his book, *The Big Drink*, E. J. Kahn of the *New Yorker* described the Coca-Cola bottler in a chapter title, "The Most Important Businessman in Town." The fame of the product, the business, and the bottle itself are all the more remarkable considering the fact that Asa G. Candler, the company's founder, arrived in Atlanta with just $1.75 to his name and that mere sugar, carbonated water, and the storied secret ingredient 7X form the basis of the product. The Coca-Cola family is careful not to claim any magical properties for the drink, describing it merely as delicious and refreshing. But noted American editor William Allen White of Emporia, Kansas, went a step further, classifying it as "the sublimated essence of all America stands for, a decent thing honestly made and typical of the average American town; too big for a hamlet, too small for a city, the breeding ground for the middle class."[2]

In the words of one college president praising a bottling enterprise in LaGrange-West Point, the bottling system was a "tributary to a golden stream."[3] As The Coca-Cola Company benefitted from sale of the syrup to the bottlers, the franchisees prospered in like measure, and then shared their prosperity with the residents of their territories. The system served as an engine of growth locally, and investors who backed the enterprise became wealthy. The beverage gained favor among consumers first on Main Street and ultimately on Wall Street as it became the world's favorite refreshment.

When The Coca-Cola Company started buying back many of the franchised bottling plants during the 1970s and 1980s, the rewards reaped by the company were tremendous. In a front-page story on 20 October 1997, just two days after the death of Coca-Cola Company CEO Roberto C. Goizueta, *The Wall Street Journal* showed how in Goizueta's sixteen years of running the company the value of Coke stock rose from $4 billion to $145 billion. The result was "a rise that has spread prosperity through Coke's home state of Georgia...."[4]

The Wall Street Journal followed on 24 October 1997, with yet another singular tribute captioned, "Bill Clinton? He Was President in The Goizueta Era." Presidents of the nation count for less than they used to, the piece stated, adding that "such a corporate chieftain with vision...can have a larger impact on the world than even a two-term President."[5]

Yet while Goizueta's impact was enormous, he almost certainly would have acknowledged the contributions of those on whose foundations he built and on whose shoulders he stood. People such as Robert W. Woodruff, Asa G. Candler, and the franchise families who helped launch the bottling system in Georgia: The Montgomerys of Atlanta, the Barrons of Rome, the Robertses of Columbus, the Samses of Athens, the Haleys of Albany, and the Cobbs of LaGrange-West Point.[6] And, although over the state line, one cannot leave out the pair of entrepreneurs from Chattanooga, Tennessee—Benjamin F. Thomas and Joseph B. Whitehead (later joined by John T. Lupton)—who initiated the bottling franchise system.[7] The following chapters are intended to highlight some of these personalities who made the product a virtual way of life along the highways and byways of twentieth-century Georgia.

While responsible for the obvious task of supplying bottled Coca-Cola, the syrup supplier praised the bottlers for their other contributions as well. Coca-Cola Company President Asa G. Candler (who initially thought the product should remain a soda fountain refreshment) was prompted in the January 1911 edition of *The Bottler* to write: "I cannot refrain from expressing my cordial appreciation of the high character of men who represent the bottling department of this corporation through the country. I find them actively associated with commercial bodies, lending their help toward building up the material and moral interests in their localities. Generally, they are officially connected with some church, and are depended upon for active, useful service in connection with church influences and purposes...."[8]

Indeed, with the bottler body as a whole, a new gospel was being preached and practiced. And while some might say it was the gospel of wealth this new breed proclaimed, it also was a faith in which adherents found ways to build up their communities and home-based institutions, and for this latter practice they had outstanding role models in Woodruff and Candler of Big Coke. Good citizenship and extensive philanthropy were the rule at all levels of the industry, rather than the exception. As Kahn stated in *The Big Drink*, "Throughout the South there is ample evidence, much of it sheathed in marble, of the civic spirit of Coca-Cola men and women."[9]

Beginning with the first bottling franchise in Chattanooga in 1899 and a second in Atlanta in 1900, there were 1,000 plants authorized to conduct business by 1919. (The total stood at about 1,100 by 1959, but there are little more than one hundred ownerships today.) To establish bottling plants and the communities they served in a symbiotic relationship, the operations were built on the bedrock of localism and as closely identified with their constituencies as Main Street itself. (It hurt nothing, the franchisees will tell you, that the parent entity's great leader, Robert W. Woodruff, decreed, "We want every-body who has to do with this product to make money."[10]) Almost everywhere Coca-Cola bottlers were soon arriving among the commercial-cultural elite of their communities.

In recent years, however, with The Coca-Cola Company's acquisition of the vast majority of such franchises, a way of conducting business and a philosophy of citizenship largely have disappeared. It was as though Main Street had been replaced by an interstate highway or a shopping mall. A more mobile consumer base and greater economies of scale in distribution are among the more discernible differences in the current scheme of bottling business, an industry whose two top companies claim about eighty percent of all soft drink sales. In a study of the economies of this business, *Competition and Concentration*, Robert D. Tollison and his co-authors sum up the current state of affairs. "Both...have integrated vertically since the late 1970s by purchasing bottling and franchise rights, suggesting that the two major concentrate producers believe that there are in-firm advantages from owning bottlers rather contracting with them for various services." As one old-line Coca-Cola man remarked, "We believed that you had to know the territory, and the system worked. I'm not saying we did a better job in the old days; it's just different now and it *is* working."[11]

The working relationship between the Coca-Cola bottler network and The Coca-Cola Company is a unique one that requires some explanation. A Coca-Cola Company publication explains it well:

> In order to withstand the inevitable bottling competition the Atlanta-based Coca-Cola Bottlers Association was established in 1914 and continues today to provide a diverse range of programs for the collective benefit of its members. Atlanta banker Ernest Woodruff and a group of investors purchased The Coca-Cola Company in 1919 from Asa Candler, who had bought Dr. John Styth Pemberton's rights in 1888. Robert Winship Woodruff was elected President. Under his creative management and strong leadership, the Company soared to unprecedented commercial success throughout the world. Today, Coca-Cola products are sold to approximately five billion customers and consumers who live in over 185 countries and enjoy almost 670 million Coca-Cola pro-

ducts every day. The bottling system is the world's largest production and distribution network.[12]

This explanation would seem to be rather straightforward and simple, but in fact the parent-bottler relationship over the past 100 years has been a complicated web of sometime-conflicting aims and interests based on several factors and circumstances.

Among those considerations:

- when and under what delimiting circumstances were particular franchises awarded;
- prevailing weather and climatic conditions especially in the days before widespread air conditioning;
- family ties whereby an assortment of kinfolk owned a piece of one or more franchises;
- the politics of bottler connections with various parent company leaders; and
- the world price of sugar.

By the time business writers, for their part, began to give voice to what was becoming the conventional wisdom about a business success story entering its second century, Chairman Goizueta began to speak of inventing a new corporate culture. Such declarations and changes did not universally endear him to industry analysts, bottlers, or employees. As *Fortune*'s Thomas Moore pointed out, "Most of Coke's bottling franchises, the backbone of its distribution system, used to be owned by entrepreneurs who had exclusive rights to bottle and sell Coca-Cola products in specific territories." He pointed out that the system worked fine for years, but as the cola wars heated up the late 1970s, "bottlers' efficiency became more important than ever to building, or in Coke's case holding, market share." By then, leveraged buyout artists were drawn to the action as third- and fourth-generation owners began to sell off their franchises. The parent company's response was to buy in themselves and to discover, in the words of one bottler, "They can make more money from bottling the product and selling it than they could from just by selling the syrup to their bottlers." Achieving economies of scale came to be the order of the day in the soft drink business. Some bottlers had seen the handwriting on the wall as early as 1986, expressing fear to the trade press that the company would no longer need the bottler network.[13]

IN 1899, TWO CHATTANOOGA BUSINESSMEN, JOSEPH B. Whitehead and Benjamin F. Thomas, came to the president of The Coca-Cola Company, Asa G. Candler, with an idea that Candler considered harebrained at best. The men related that they wished they could enjoy Coca-Cola ice-cold at the baseball park, and asked if they could gain bottling rights to the popular new drink on a wide scale basis. As he recalled the conversation years later, Candler said his answer was to the effect that he had "neither the money, the time, or the brains to embark in the bottling business." He supposedly added, "There are too many who are not responsible, who care nothing about the reputation of what they put up, and I am afraid the name will be injured."[14]

Later, on 21 July of the same year, the Tennesseans persuaded Candler to let them go ahead with the project, with no charge for the rights he gave away. Mark Pendergrast, in his unauthorized history of Coca-Cola, *For God, Country, and Coca-Cola*, labeled the 600-word contract the parties signed "the world's stupidest, smartest contract." At any rate, Chattanooga's minor league baseball team soon had the beverage on sale, courtesy of the two men and another partner, J. T. Lupton, who joined the duo after the signing. Before long Georgia-based bottlers were in the business, as well.[15]

The emphasis upon the product's mobility, learned by assiduously cultivating sales at sporting events, such as at the Chattanooga Lookouts' games, opened up other possibilities when it came to expanding the industry. Bottled Coke would soon go to the cruise ships and motion picture houses, to the beaches and resorts, and to industrial plants and theaters of war. The company's and the bottlers' goal was expressed in the advertising tag line, "Always within an arm's length of desire." One of the company's leaders would sum up the challenge this way, "What," he asked, "can you and I do to make Coca-Cola available to anyone, anywhere in the world, whenever they want one, and be certain that it tastes just like the last Coca-Cola they drank?" This was The Great Commission for the Coca-Cola business, and once put into practice by company and bottler alike, Main Street interconnected with the global economy.[16]

WHILE THEIR SUCCESS MAY HAVE MADE THEM THE kings of all they surveyed, Robert W. Woodruff and Asa G. Candler spoke the language of Main Street Georgia and were never far removed from the bottlers, who in diverse ways remained neighbors and lifelong friends. Candler, brother of the Methodist bishop of Georgia, contributed land and money to bring Emory University to Atlanta. In addition, he served as mayor of the city, and during a time of severe financial distress advanced Atlanta's city government some $300,000. Robert W. Woodruff was Georgia's largest landowner and a great benefactor to Atlanta's art scene.[17] He also was the Sunday School pupil of Asa G. Candler and donated more than $225 million to Emory University. (The grand total of Woodruff's philanthropy approximated $340 million.) A portion of that total once represented the largest philanthropic gift on record.[18]

Demonstrably, the per-capita contribution in civic service, community leadership, and funding from many of the bottlers and parent company figures in Georgia made a great difference on the state's Main Streets. These towns loved their Coke men and women. As an editorial said of W. C. Bradley of Columbus, a commanding figure in the leadership of Coca-Cola and the affairs of that West Georgia city, upon his death: "He in every sense of the word was our very own." The Barron legacy was accorded unique recognition, as well, when the original franchise holder, Frank S. Barron, died in September 1935. The announcer on radio station WRGA opened with these words, "The heart of all Rome is sadder tonight" and went on to lament how the city would miss Barron's "willingness to lend a helping hand, his sterling character, and absolute integrity." Noting that "all Rome loved Frank Barron and its heart is bowed down in genuine sorrow," the announcer closed with the declaration, "His hand was to be found in every effort for the good of his home and community. He loved Rome and Rome loved him." The spirit alluded to by the announcer was the same spirit of community that prompted Barron to appear unannounced at a grieving family's back door and silently leave a case of Coca-Cola. It was a ritual of friendship and appreciation repeated countless times.[19]

Sports Go Better with Coke

GEORGIA BOTTLERS TYPICALLY JOINED WITH the parent company to help underwrite any deficit the University of Georgia incurred as the Bulldogs football team traveled to play Yale and other Eastern powers, such as Dartmouth and New York University. These same bottlers also contributed heavily to sponsorship of the Georgia Bulldog games on a statewide radio hook-up, as well as to the school's Vince Dooley Library Fund.[20]

My own father, once a high school football coach and superintendent, solemnly advised his ten-year-old, "Son, play football for Georgia, and you'll get a job with Coca-Cola!" I took the advice, announcing Bulldog sports, and evidently that was good enough to land a job with the soft drink giant.[21]

In minor league sports, as well, Georgia's bottlers played a lead role. The Southern Baseball Association's Atlanta Crackers, long known as the most successful of minor league franchises, for many years was owned and controlled by Coca-Cola interests in the Peach State. So, it was none too surprising that in 1965 Atlanta Coca-Cola Bottling Company President Arthur Montgomery mobilized the Atlanta forces that took the city to the major leagues, capturing both the Atlanta Braves and the Atlanta

---

Falcons. Of course, Coca-Cola was granted an exclusive for the sale of soft drinks in Atlanta Stadium.[22]

WHAT THE COCA-COLA BUSINESS IN GEORGIA HAS lost, principally in terms of good will and community identification, and what is has gained as a result of radical changes in the pattern of its bottling operations, will be determined on another day, but not likely in some corporate boardroom. Rather, the verdict may come in local gathering places, such as the Partridge Restaurant in Rome or at high school concession stands in Albany. As one bottling company presi-dent, H. B. Nicholson, a former schoolteacher and a native of Richland, Georgia, opened in a speech to bottlers in 1945: "Men, I am telling you that one item of good will which you place at one dollar is worth more by far than all the physical assets which that balance sheet contains." [23]

Endnotes

[1] Frederick Allen, *Secret Formula: How Brilliant Marketing and Relentless Salesmanship Made Coca-Cola the Best Known Product in the World* (New York: Harper Business, 1994); Thomas Oliver, *The Real Coke, The Real Story* (New York: Random House, 1986) 18.

[2] E. J. Kahn, *The Big Drink* (New York: Random House, 1960) 69-81, 117-118; H. B. Nicholson, "Host to Thirsty Main Street," speech to the Newcomen Society in North America, New York, 18 December 1953.

[3] Waights G. Henry, *Tributary to a Golden Stream: The Story of the Coca-Cola Bottling Company of West Point-LaGrange, Georgia* (New York: Newcomen Society in North America, 1982).

[4] Nikhil Deogun, "The Legacy: Roberto Goizueta Led Coca-Cola Surge, and Its Home Prospers; He Said Social Good Came with Creating Wealth," *Wall Street Journal*, 20 October 1997, A1.

[5] Gary Pomerantz, "Atlanta's GROWTH Stock: One Miracle After Another, Success of Coca-Cola Has Fueled Surge in Assets," *Atlanta Journal-Constitution*, 22 October 1995, H7; Paul A. Gigot, "Bill Clinton? He was President in the Goizueta Era," *Wall Street Journal*, 24 October 1997, A22.

[6] As a measure of the influence of these Georgia franchise holders in the Coca-Cola business, three of them were featured speakers on the program of the first bottlers convention in 1909. They were Arthur Montgomery of Atlanta, W. B. Haley of Albany, and Columbus Roberts of Columbus. From the very early days of the bottler network, The Coca-Cola Company developed several outstanding inspirational speakers who entertained, informed, and persuaded its franchisees. And the bottlers came to eagerly anticipate that feature of company-bottler meetings. *The Coca-Cola Bottler*, December 1959.

[7] Chattanooga has long been the object of several "bitter border battles" between Georgia and Tennessee. In 1893, the Colonial Dames noted that "Georgia again appointed a boundary commission, without satisfactory results, and there is still feeling that some of its territory is wrongfully under the jurisdiction of the state of Tennessee." Commissioners from the respective states had met in 1818 and established a boundary, but for whatever reason the

agreement never was ratified and the property in question returned to Georgia. As late as 1942 a threat was made to create a new state line, which would place Chattanooga in north Georgia. See "Bitter Border Battles," *The Historical News*, June 1998; Elfrida DeRenne Barrow, et al, *Georgia: A Pageant of Years* (Spartanburg SC: The Reprint Company, 1974) 176; and Marion R. Hemperly and Edwin L. Jackson, *Georgia's Boundaries: The Shaping of a State* (Athens: Carl Vinson Institute of Government/University of Georgia, 1993) 43-44, 88-90.

[8] Asa G. Candler, Message from the President, *The Coca-Cola Bottler*, January 1911.

[9] Kahn, *The Big Drink*, 85.

[10] H. B. Nicholson, "Coke's First 100 Years," *Beverage World* (April 1986) advertisement, unnumbered page; Gerald Imlay, *The Coca-Cola Bottlers Association*, interview by author, Atlanta, Georgia, 30 May 1995; Jeannie Woodley, The Coca-Cola Company, interview by author, Atlanta, Georgia, 30 May 1995. Imlay and Woodley identify only two independent bottlers remaining in Georgia, those in Thomasville and Milledgeville; the other territories in the state are owned by three "mega bottlers:" Coca-Cola Enterprises, Atlanta; Coca-Cola Bottling Consolidated, Charlotte; and Coca-Cola Bottling Company United, Birmingham. These ownerships do well in excess of eighty percent of The Coca-Cola Company's total U.S. concentrate volume. See also Kahn, *The Big Drink*, 82.

[11] Robert D. Tollison, David P. Kaplan, Richard S. Higgins, *Competition and Concentration* (Lexington MA: Lexington Books, 1986), introduction, 77; W. Frank Barron, interview by author, Rome, Georgia, 17 March 1993.

[12] "A Brief History of The Coca-Cola Company and Bottling System," *Coca-Cola Scholars Foundation Annual Report* (Atlanta: The Coca-Cola Company, 1993). This publication is distributed by The Coca-Cola Scholars Foundation in connection with its scholarship program for high school students, the largest such undertaking known to American enterprise. The foundation is jointly funded by The Coca-Cola Bottlers Association, headquartered a few miles from the parent company in Atlanta, and The Coca-Cola Company itself.

[13] Thomas Moore, "He Put the Kick Back in Coke," *Fortune*, 26 October 1987, 47; Sanders Rowland, interview by author, Asheville, North Carolina, 17 March 1987; Jack Bernabucci, president, Coca-

Cola Bottling Co. of Jamestown, North Dakota, interview published in *Beverage World: Coke's First 100 Years*, April 1986, 226-228.

[14] Kahn, *The Big Drink*, 82.

[15] Mark Pendergrast, *For God, For Country, and Coca-Cola* (New York: Scribner's, 1993) 72-84.

[16] Charles Elliott, *Mr. Anonymous* (Atlanta: Cherokee Publishing Company, 1982) 126.

[17] Sam Heys, "Woodruff Helped Make Atlanta What It is Today," *The Atlanta Constitution*, 7 May 1986, C4. The philanthropist never tried to put on airs when it came to his support of the beaux arts; Atlanta architect George T. Heery tells of asking Woodruff his opinion of the multi-million dollar Heery-designed Woodruff Arts Center and getting the folksy evaluation, "Pretty swanky." George T. Heery, interview by author, Highlands, North Carolina, 17 July 1991.

[18] *Beverage World*, 118; Bob Hall, "Coca-Cola and Methodism," *Southern Exposure* (1977): 98-101. Coca-Cola and Methodism, by the way, had a distinct connection, one not stemming entirely from the kinship of Asa G. Candler and brother Warren A. Candler, the bishop. In fact, by far the largest benefactors of Georgia Methodism have been Woodruff, Candler, and other key Coca-Cola individuals.

[19] *Columbus Ledger-Enquirer*, 27 July 1947, 8; *The Coca-Cola Bottler*, November 1935, 29-30.

[20] Chantel Dunham, Development Office, University of Georgia, interview by author, Athens, Georgia, 25 May 1995.

[21] Mike Cheatham, *Class of the Carolinas* (Asheville NC: Bee Tree Books, 1992) 58-59.

[22] Furman Bisher, *Miracle in Atlanta* (Cleveland OH: World Publishing Company, 1966) 27-28. Three decades later, the Olympic committee of Greece (hosts to the first Olympic Games in 1886) insisted that The Coca-Cola Company stole the 1996 Centennial Olympic Games for Atlanta, according to *Atlanta Journal-Constitution* staff writer Ailene Voisin (26 June 1995, D8).

[23] Harry Jacobs, Book Reviews, *The American Spectator*, April 1995, 62-63; H. B. Nicholson, *The Coca-Cola Bottler* (Atlanta: Hickory Publishing Company, 1945) 52.

2

THE CHATTANOOGA BOTTLERS

In 1899, Chattanooga lawyers Benjamin F. Thomas and Joseph B. Whitehead were drawn to the bustling city of Atlanta. The city had played host to the Piedmont Exposition just a few years prior, and more recently to the Cotton States and International Exposition, drawing the nation's attention to the "Chicago of the South."[1] No Atlanta booster—of which there were many—could fail to admire the enterprise and boldness of Thomas and Whitehead. (There is nothing a good salesman so admires as another one.) Their goal: to convince a reluctant Asa Candler to grant them the rights to bottle and distribute Coca-Cola.

ATLANTA HISTORIAN AND AUTHOR FRANKLIN MILLER Garrett once worked for The Coca-Cola Company, with positions in its advertising and industry relations department and as the company historian. As such, Garrett is the perfect person to explain the story of the two pioneering Chattanoogans (and of John T. Lupton, a colleague of the two who later bought part of Whitehead's interest) who obtained bottling rights from Asa G. Candler and franchised them across the country, setting in motion the legacy of Georgia's bottlers. The story of these men ranks with railroads among his favorite topics, and he was happy to tell it during a 1998 meeting.[2]

"I think Mr. Thomas and Mr. Whitehead would have taken the old Western & Atlantic—the State Road, as it was called since it was owned outright by the state of Georgia and actually has some valuable property in downtown Chattanooga." The length of the journey? "One hundred and thirty miles each way." And how long a ride was it? "Exactly five hours and thirty-five minutes, assuming they took the day express." In all likelihood, although Garrett has not been able to substantiate it, they stayed at The Arlington on Marietta Street. Garrett even espouses on the dining car they might have used, "A good one!" he exclaims.[3]

With permission granted from The Coca-Cola Company, the following is an excerpt from Garrett's more extensive history, prepared for the company, chronicling the rise of these early bottlers:

About [1899], Thomas and Whitehead came to a realization that it would not be possible, financially or physically, for them personally to blanket the country with bottling plants. They had the obligation under their contract with Mr. Candler to supply the demand for bottled Coca-Cola in the territory comprising almost the entire United States; and it became immediately apparent that it would be necessary, in order for them to discharge their obligation, to subcontract the right to bottle Coca-Cola to private investors throughout the country.

Thereupon they began, with the approval of The Coca-Cola Company, a search for qualified individuals willing to invest their own capital in return for the exclusive right to bottle and sell Coca-Cola within a specific territory. The incentive provided by the grant of an exclusive territory, coupled with the license to make use of the trademark, was destined to boot-strap a virtually non-existing business into a major industry in U.S. commerce. The initial investments by the first Bottlers, though modest by today's standards, often represented the total resources of the original Bottlers. The product had at that time attained only modest celebrity, and the task of enlisting qualified bottlers throughout the country was a formidable one. As a result, it was necessary to assure the Bottler that he would have the exclusive right to bottle and sell Coca-Cola in the particular territory in return for the Bottler's agreement to make the investment in resources and effort that was required to carry out the obligations of the original grant from Mr. Candler....

Not long afterward, as a result of amicable differences between the Messrs. Thomas and Whitehead, they split their large domain. The partners agreed that Whitehead would make the geographical division and that Thomas would have his choice of the two resulting areas. He chose the heavily populated segment of the country, still, for the most part, included in the territory of The Coca-Cola Bottling Company (Thomas) Inc., plus the states of California, Oregon, and Washington. Thomas elected to stay in Chattanooga; Whitehead moved to Atlanta in 1900, and Lupton remained in Chattanooga as the equal partner of Whitehead.

In April 1900, Joe Whitehead secured a permit from the City of Atlanta to open a bottling plant and went into operation of the southeast corner of Edgewood Avenue and Courtland Street for the summer season. This original Atlanta operation, progenitor of The Atlanta Coca-Cola Bottling Company, was a joint enterprise of J. B. Whitehead and J. T. Lupton. Whitehead was the active manager until 1903, when Arthur Montgomery of the old Southern Express Company purchased a third interest and took over active management....

In 1901, Ben Thomas sold The Coca-Cola Bottling Works of Chattanooga to his friends, James F. Johnston and William H. Hardin. It is reasonably certain that these men became the first operating bottling plant owners under the 1899 contract, after original grantees Thomas and Whitehead.

President Asa G. Candler, of The Coca-Cola Company, must have been pleased indeed at the zeal displayed by the two insistent young men to whom he had granted bottling rights in 1899. During the following decade, 379 plants had been put into operation, inspiring J. J. Willard, then at Philadelphia and a relative of Candler, to launch, in 1909, a new magazine which he named *The Coca-Cola Bottler.*

As the search for local Bottlers met with increasing success, administrative responsibilities grew apace. It soon became apparent to Whitehead and Lupton that they both had physical and financial limitations. They could never hope to adequately serve their territory directly as actual Bottlers and, in addition, act as "franchisers" to others who would be granted contracts to process and sell Coca-Cola locally in specified territory.

And so, they divided their large domain into three separate areas, supervised by three separate companies whose sole function was to issue contracts authorizing locally owned and operated companies to process or bottle and market Coca-Cola with the knowledge and consent of The Coca-Cola Company.

The arrangement was akin to the old familiar one of "Wholesaler" and "Retailer." Whitehead and Lupton, as "Wholesalers," purchased Coca-Cola syrup from The Coca-Cola Company and sold it to the local bottling companies which became "Retailers" in processing or bottling and marketing the finished product, Coca-Cola.

The designation "Parent Bottler" was chosen in lieu of the more ambiguous "Wholesaler." So was born the distributional structure which was destined to serve for so long and so effectively the manufacturing and marketing needs of a unique new enterprise.

And thusly came into being the four Parent Bottling Companies: The Coca-Cola Bottling Company, with headquarters in Atlanta; The Coca-Cola Bottling Company (1903), with offices in Dallas, Texas; the Western Coca-Cola Bottling Company, headquartered in Chicago; and The Coca-Cola Bottling Company (Thomas), Inc., in Chattanooga....

By the time the First World War ended, the entire continental United States was being served by Coca-Cola Bottlers. In 1919, their number was 1,000. Individual Bottlers, during the intervening years, have made tremendous strides. Practically all plants have moved from obscure locations on back or side streets to prominent sites. Many have become local show places. Machinery, originally operated by hand or foot power, has become largely automatic. Delivery equipment has progressed from the plodding horse and wagon to primitive chain-driven trucks to streamlined motorized equipment. Many plants [were later] operated by the third and fourth generations from the founding fathers.

Not the least interesting aspect of historical inquiry is speculation—speculation as to what might have happened had not a particular event occurred. Indeed, at this point in this account of The Coca-Cola Company, the question arises as to what might have happened to the soft drink industry had Asa G. Candler not given bottling rights (for one dollar of which there is no record of collection) to Benjamin F. Thomas and Joseph B. Whitehead, but instead retained them....

But Candler did transfer the bottling rights as already described, and Whitehead and Thomas assumed the obligation to build bottling plants adequate to supply the demand for Coca-Cola throughout the United States. Unable to do so by means of their own efforts and financial resources, Thomas and Whitehead and their successors thus created hundreds of local businesses by granting licenses, territory by territory to men of character and enterprise who were willing to make the investment and to sacrifice and labor in order to build up their enterprise....[4]

The Familiar Green Bottle

IN THE EARLY YEARS OF THE TWENTIETH century the shape and color of the Coca-Cola bottle varied from territory to territory. But Ben Thomas recognized the need for consistency throughout the territories, stating: "We need a bottle which a person can recognize as a Coca-Cola bottle when he feels it in the dark. It should be so shaped that, even if broken it would be recognized at a glance for what it is."

Harold Hirsch, general counsel for The Coca-Cola Company, agreed. In July 1913, Hirsch wrote to all bottlers and to The Coca-Cola Company "urging the development and adoption of a uniform and distinctive package for Coca-Cola." An Indiana glass manufacturer heeded the call, and by 1915 a design was patented. Since that time Coke's distinctive bottle has become a universal symbol of refreshment.[5]

MILLIONS OF AMERICANS HAVE GOOD MEMORIES OF their "friendly, hometown neighbor who bottles Coca-Cola" (as the tag line for the advertising once ran). They remember the bottling plant on their hometown main streets. And they associate the distinctive taste with some special moments in their lives.[6] And while the number of independent franchisees has declined in recent times (there are only about 100 remaining; some forty years ago there were about 1,100), the good works and exceptional corporate citizenship that were service marks can be seen today in the many charitable foundations these franchises have spawned. And there are few better exemplars of this legacy than the foundations of the Thomas, Whitehead, and Lupton families.

A century after Thomas and Whitehead set out by rail for Atlanta and their fateful meeting with Candler, their city of Chattanooga has embarked on a course of rescuing the old and crumbling manufacturing center. According to the *Atlanta Journal-Constitution*, by 1969 Chattanooga had earned from the federal government, for its belching smokestacks and polluted waterfront, an ignominious title, "the dirtiest city in America." But by 1988, the city had met federal Clean Air Act standards. The Atlanta daily saw what Chattanooga resolved to do and commented: "To be sure post-Olympic Atlanta has a long list of revitalization plans of its own. But its smaller neighbor to the north, an industrial wasteland a decade ago, has demonstrated a much-heralded wherewithal to bring its vision for its future to reality and has become a model for other cities trying to rejuvenate downtowns."[7]

The driving force behind all of this? "The deep pockets of civic-minded philanthropists," the Atlanta article states, namely the Lyndhurst and Benwood Foundations. Lyndhurst was created to honor the memory of J. T. Lupton by son Cartter Lupton; Benwood sprang from the philanthropy of Benjamin Thomas and his nephew and successor, George Thomas Hunter. The two are among the largest charitable foundations in Tennessee, their combined assets comfortably exceeding $200 million. And while more will be said of these progressive entities and their programs of work in the final chapter, their evolution and leadership must be emphasized.[8]

The lead article of *The Chattanooga Times* on 3 October 1950 disclosed that George Thomas Hunter had left his entire holdings in The Coca-Cola Bottling Company (Thomas), Inc. to the Benwood Foundation. Only recently, however, has the foundation begun to accept recognition for its good works. (That policy was in character with the Coca-Cola men and women whom had a natural reticence and did not seek the praise of their neighbors.) *The Chattanooga Times* piece added, "No Chattanoogan ever left so large a fortune to be used for the purposes which Hunter outlined in the by-laws of the corporation organized to administer the trust." Benwood was to disperse funds in perpetuity to "religious, scientific, literary and educational activities as will promote the advancement or well-being of mankind."[9]

Hunter, who was brought in by his uncle to learn the business, became Thomas's heir. And on founding Benwood the nephew said of the foundation, "It will be my heir." The current president of Benwood is Sebert Brewer Jr., whose late father was a founding trustee and served as chairman and president of The Coca-Cola Bottling Company (Thomas), Inc. Brewer relates the commonly accepted story of the test Hunter would apply when faced with a decision about supporting a given cause. He simply asked himself what his predecessor and uncle, Ben Thomas, would do. If the answer was, "Ben would," then Benwood would lend support.[10]

Soon after Ben Thomas and Joe Whitehead returned with the franchising contract, the first advertisement for bottled Coca-Cola appeared in Chattanooga. "Drink a bottle of Coca-Cola, five cents at all stands, grocers and saloons." To say that the invitation was enthusiastically greeted, of course, would be a gross understatement. As a report issued on the occasion of Benwood's fiftieth anniversary stated, "Ben Thomas's dream was realized through the success stories of the family of franchise bottling operations." The report explains further that these were labor intensive, dependable sources of employment—something of considerable pride not only to the chamber of commerce but to the community at large. After all, "Coca-Cola bottlers would earn the reputation of being exemplary citizens.... Boy Scout troops, football teams, churches, schools, and hospitals could count on the generous support of the local Coke bottler." And so they did, in Chattanooga and throughout Georgia.[11]

Endnotes

[1] Richard Funderburke, "Architect and Entrepreneur: G. L. Normann and Atlanta's Great Fairs," *Atlanta History* XLI (1997) 5-21.

[2] Garrett is much beloved by the citizens of Atlanta and the patrons of the Atlanta History Center, where even at the age of ninety-three he still comes into work almost daily. An Atlanta resident since 1914, he can answer virtually any question about the city and its environs. See Doris Lockerman, *The Man Who Amazed Atlanta: The Journey of Franklin Miller Garrett* (Atlanta: Longstreet Press, 1996).

[3] Franklin M. Garrett, interview by author, Atlanta, Georgia, 30 January 1998.

[4] *The Coca-Cola Company: An Illustrated Profile of a Worldwide Company* (Atlanta: The Coca-Cola Company, 1974) 24-30.

[5] *The Coca-Cola Company: An Illustrated Profile*, 28-29.

[6] Based on response to author's request for information, memories, and photographs concerning Georgia's bottlers. Request appeared in *Farmers and Consumers Market Bulletin*, 29 July 1998.

[7] Melissa Turner, "Pardon Me, Boys, is THIS Chattanooga?", *Atlanta Journal-Constitution*, 20 April 1998, E1. See also Brendan I. Koerner, *U.S. News and World Report*, 8 June 1998, 26-27, 31-32; and Paula Couch Thrasher, "Chattanooga's Riverfront Renaissance," *Atlanta Journal-Constitution*, 13 December 1998, L1.

[8] Melissa Turner, E1; 1995 Annual Report (Chattanooga TN: The Benwood Foundation, 1996); and *The Foundation Directory* (New York: The Foundation Center, 1995) 1412, 1421.

[9] *The Chattanooga Times*, 3 October 1950, 1; Benwood Foundation Annual Report.

[10] Sebert Brewer Jr., interview by author, Chattanooga, Tennessee, 26 June 1998.

[11] Benwood Foundation Annual Report.

3

THE MONTGOMERY FAMILY
OF ATLANTA

Start not chronologically, but with the last man in the
Montgomery clan to head up the Atlanta Coca-Cola Bottling
Company. That's Arthur L. Montgomery, described by
Atlanta author Pat Watters in 1979 as "a dapper middle-aged
man, a third-generation bottler." Then, to echo a remark often
heard about Montgomery, "courteous and genial in a no-
nonsense sort of way."[1] Furman Bisher, too, in profiling one
of "the big three" who brought major league sports to Atlanta
in the mid-1960s, called him "a forceful man in his forties."[2]

Montgomery is a valued and involved community leader.
He has met with notable success in a number of business
ventures unrelated to his bread and butter — Coca-Cola. And,
according to The Coca-Cola Company Vice President who
related to bottlers of the product in the Southeast, "Arthur and
his operation were the very essence of what we in the
business called 'the quality image.'"[3]

A generation of Coca-Cola people and emerging business
leaders related to him, it seems, and admired the flair he
displayed in bringing to fruition a civic project or a business
undertaking. Montgomery had a way of calling both peers
and younger colleagues by name while serving as a problem

solver for one of the fifty-or-so groups on whose boards he sat, or socializing at an industry gathering. At the same time, Montgomery brought energy and vision to the Atlanta chamber's "Forward Atlanta" campaign, which prompted 450 of the Fortune 500 companies to set up for business in his city.[4]

In addition to his pro-bono service, the young executive was once part owner of Atlanta's ABC-TV affiliate and was a director of Life of Georgia. Always relied upon by his colleagues in The Coca-Cola Bottlers Association for his sound judgment in the area of marketing, he was the association's chairman for advertising and frequently was sought out for advice by The Coca-Cola Company and its advertising agency. For the Cooperative Advertising Program, which pooled the resources of some 1,100 bottlers with those of the parent company, Montgomery represented the bottler's viewpoint.[5]

As chairman of Atlanta's Stadium Authority, he was a man with a mission, as well: the city would go big league with major league sports franchises. An October 1964 article by Bill Diehl incorporated the thoughts of the article's title: "The Story of the Man, the Stadium, the Braves and Things Which Just Go Better With Him in Charge." The writer observed that "the stadium job is a gigantic chore, yet Arthur Montgomery is going about it with the same relaxed, easy-going attitude with which he attacks all of his responsibilities." In further praise of the Coca-Cola bottler's style, the writer adds, "He moves with the casual self-assurance of a man accustomed to just getting it done."[6]

The man inspired trust in his peers, as well as an emerging generation of civic leadership. "I remember when I was grass green and just started work at The Coca-Cola

Bottlers Association," says Jerry Imlay. "Arthur had me over to tour the Spring Street plant and welcomed me so cordially; same thing on Sunday mornings at North Avenue Presbyterian Church, where I ushered." Another man, then a young executive at The Coca-Cola Company, remembers how the bottler always would answer his own telephone. ("I learned that from the banker, Mills B. Lane Jr., who had that practice," chuckles Montgomery. "Mills always said his secretary was a lot more busy than he was.") Adds another longtime Montgomery associate, speaking of both Montgomery and the city's Mayor Ivan Allen: "They were brisk, handsome, intelligent—the kind of people who made us realize we could accomplish about anything in this state." He adds, "that pair showed us the way, and we were convinced there was nothing we couldn't aspire to and achieve."[7]

Officers at the parent entity often would tap the Atlanta bottler for board service or an important public appearance representing Coca-Cola business. "Heck, Arthur makes a lot better impression than most of us around here," was one vice-president's assessment.[8] While Robert W. Woodruff would consent to be photographed with future network anchor Diane Sawyer, the 1963 "America's Junior Miss" (the pageant sponsored annually for a number of years by the company and its bottlers), it was Montgomery who would be snapped, say, with the cast of Billy Wilder's 1961 farce, *One, Two, Three*. (The classic portrayed James Cagney as the Coca-Cola bottler for West Germany, who sought to invade Soviet Russia with the ideal capitalistic beverage for the masses.)

Why did "Monty"—as sports pages of the Atlanta dailies sometimes called him—seek to perpetuate the earlier-mentioned 'quality image' so assiduously cultivated by earlier generations of the Montgomery family? Why was good corporate citizenship such a priority? "It 'came with the territory,'" explains the man who practically wrote the book about bottler psychology, Jim Wimberly. "For one thing, I remember that the Atlanta plant had life-sized metal figures of a smiling policeman at all the school crossings, reminding drivers to slow down—that's just one way they showed they cared about the schools and the children," Wimberly said. Too, the Montgomery operations went so far as to send route trucks to children's homemade drink stands, donating product to the budding, young entrepreneurs. In addition to his duties in production, Arthur started as a route man on one of those runs. "They taught a kid how a business operates—a good beginning for a business education."[9]

A hard-eyed look at such youth-market promotions is that they are a way to bind the youngsters to the joys of consuming Coca-Cola for years to come. So, as one might expect, the Montgomerys were foremost in the ranks of those bottlers who brought schoolchildren to witness the bottling of Coca-Cola where "Purity Lives in a House of Glass." While consuming the product fresh off the bottling line, the students were presented Coca-Cola trademarked rulers, pencils, and tablets. The practice began in 1909 and continues, with modifications, today.[10]

Arthur and brother George Montgomery represented the well-to-do third generation in the business, one begun by the first Arthur Montgomery—this Arthur's great uncle—and his partners in 1900. A former Atlanta shipping agent for Southern Express Company, the elder Arthur had the foresight—or luck, as some might have it—to put up $2,000 to buy into the new bottling franchise. L. F., Arthur's father, came into the uncle's business while still a student at Atlanta's

Boys High School. From youth until his dying day, L. F. had known little else but work. He had no hobbies, but had a demonstrated talent for handling money. Arthur, himself, began to work around the plant about age eleven, putting in forty hours each week for six dollars in pay; upon returning from military service in World War II he joined the company full time. By 1958, at age thirty-five, he had worked his way up from advertising manager to president of the concern. "I'm the same way as my dad," Arthur says. "I tried golf, dropped it, had no hobbies." Business has been his life, and his work ethic is a highly developed one. The operation he headed was always among the ten-largest metropolitan bottling operations in the nation—and invariably first among those in terms of per-capita consumption.[11]

Yet perhaps because his father was so intensely interested in the building of Atlanta and his territory—but never could cut loose enough to take a highly visible role in the process—he encouraged Arthur to do so. The son did just that—but was equally devoted to the building of the franchise. Atlanta Coca-Cola Bottling Company had a very large territory, at one time stretching across about forty of Georgia's 159 counties and populated by thirty percent to forty percent of the state's population. It could not be cultivated by an indifferent management. The Montgomerys set up subplants along the railroad lines: Gainesville, Conyers, Griffin, Marietta, Newnan, Lawrenceville, and Ballground. Other distribution points were added, and some phased out, in years to come as economies of scale were achieved. The former freight agent, Arthur the elder, had a transportation background and succeeded in great part because of that knowledge. His natural conservatism prevented him, on the other hand, from being too bullish about the business. L. F. recalled that in the early days, when the founder had reached a new high of 500 cases sold per day, he felt that things could never get better.[12]

Arthur remembers when consumer demand for the product grew so great that he had no choice but to expand his Spring Street operation. Arthur went to great pains to see that L. F., who was ill and unable to come in to the plant, was not told of the installation—the additional line cost as much as all the other equipment and the plant put together. While Arthur was worried about a violent reaction to the project, it turns out that L. F. had used a similar ploy when the first Arthur was in like circumstance.[13]

IN A LETTER A FEW YEARS AGO, FORMER MAYOR Ivan Allen reminisced about the 1930 Atlanta Crackers. That, and the way times have changed. "We've lived during possibly the greatest period of prosperity the world has ever seen," he wrote. And few who witnessed the economic miracle of a rising Atlanta during the last several decades would disagree. A 1965 newspaper article enthused over "The Big Three"—Allen, banker Mills B. Lane Jr., and Arthur Montgomery—who helped make it all happen. As with Alfred Colquitt, Joseph E. Brown, and John B. Gordon in Reconstruction Georgia, this Atlanta trio was "the new triumvirate" lifting the commercial and industrial interests of their region to new heights.[14]

What probably, as much as any single factor, symbolized the ascent was the fact that the city officially had become "big league." A gleaming new stadium was set right in the center of Atlanta and located precisely along the interstate highway en route to the new airport. After the Braves—the first of several major league franchises—chose the city, Atlanta columnist Norman Shavin conducted a poll of citizens on name ideas for the team's new stadium. The piece was lighthearted in nature, as were a good many of the suggestions offered up by respondents. "Nut Bowl" was suggested by one. "Pemberton Stadium," urged another out of respect for the creator of Coca-Cola. One Al Miller offered up the name of Arthur Montgomery, citing his role in snaring the franchise and completing the stadium in less than a year—on time and on budget. "We owe a great deal of credit and gratitude...for all his efforts in getting us the Braves."[15]

Al Thomy of the *Atlanta Constitution* wrote a lead article after the feat was accomplished, "A Doer: Montgomery Gets it Done." Murray Olderman, sports editor of the Newspaper Enterprise Association, praised the Atlanta leader to an audience of several million and even included in his column a cartoon of the bottler. Morris McLemore, sports editor of the *Miami News*, described "Monty" as a "spirited warrior for the far-flung legions of Coca-Cola." McLemore concluded, "Blood is thicker than water everywhere, but Coke is thicker than both of them in Atlanta, pal." Accolades flowed in for the leader from all directions.[16]

However, in 1979 things changed. After a dozen years as chairman of the stadium authority, Atlanta Mayor Sam Massell failed to reappoint Montgomery. Soon after the authority began its search for an administrative director—about the same time that Montgomery sold the Atlanta Coca-Cola Bottling Company. He offered to serve in the post—for just one dollar a year. His offer was refused. Picked instead was a disbarred attorney who had been convicted on tax charges. Local sports editors Furman Bisher and Jesse Outlar cried "politics" and roundly criticized city officials. The business community was up in arms. Arthur turned the other cheek.[17]

AN INTERVIEW WITH JAMES B. WILLIAMS, A prominent Atlanta banker and civic leader, provided a glowing review of Montgomery and his contributions:

A friend of mine once pointed out a photo showing Arthur Montgomery and Mayor Ivan Allen Jr. at the groundbreaking for Atlanta Stadium in 1964. They both were vigorous, handsome men—great civic leaders who were about to realize a long-held dream: major league sports for Atlanta, Georgia, and the Southeast.

The fellow said to me, "Now, Jimmy, you know those two fellows symbolized all that was good about the kind of leadership and vision we had around here in the 1960s." I agreed with him, but I think I commented that I wouldn't confine that estimate to just a single decade. Both of them have been major contributors here for a long time....

Ivan Allen believed in Henry W. Grady's idea of a New South, and he was the foremost proponent of it. That's where Arthur came in, out there negotiating with various major league teams to relocate to Atlanta. He was the indispensable man in the field. Mayor Allen said, "I nearly ran the legs off Arthur Montgomery." So I understand it was in large part Arthur who made it a done deal with the Milwaukee Braves, and here they came. The Falcons and the

Hawks soon followed. Then Arthur was named the chairman of the stadium authority and did the kind of job we knew he could.

We had seen the kind of ability Arthur had in polishing the jewel in Coca-Cola's crown, the Atlanta bottling operation. That was a well-run business, by any measure. We already had witnessed what he had accomplished with the chamber of commerce, the American Cancer Society, the Georgia alumni, and others. Arthur presented himself well wherever he went, and people just plain liked the fellow....As a good Coca-Cola Bottler, Arthur Montgomery always looked out for his territory. He took pains to cultivate and develop it, along with everything that was good for it. When Arthur's territory grew and prospered, this town and this state benefited. In his mind that was just good business. Well, I can tell you it was first-class citizenship, too.

As mild-mannered and personable as Arthur is, he is a spirited competitor. Perhaps that's why major sports made his competitive juices flow. But, you know, whenever Arthur Montgomery has won, we've won. And that ought to go into everybody's record book.[18]

One looks at photos of Arthur L. Montgomery during his city's and his business' "soaring sixties," and it's easy to see why he was so widely hailed for his contribution. Here, Sales and Marketing Executives-Atlanta honors him as their "Salesman of the Year" in 1965. There, the National Football Foundation and Hall of Fame awards him its Contribution to Amateur Football Award. He never sought such trophies, say friends and colleagues, he was simply acting out of an enlightened sense of corporate and community leadership. But he continues to this day to act out of that same sense of what is right for the territory, his neighborhood, his neck of the woods. In 1994 Arthur and Julie Purvis Montgomery were honored by the College of Veterinary Medicine at the University of Georgia for funding the college's Equine Locomotory Center, a facility for examining horses with lameness problems. In 1976 *Atlanta* magazine designated him one of the two hundred "Atlantans who have contributed most to the welfare, quality of life, good reputation or social conscience of the broader community during Atlanta's history." He chaired a dedicated band of civic movers in Atlanta Landmarks, Inc. to save Atlanta's storied Fox Theatre from the wrecking ball and succeeded in having the treasure designated a National Historical Landmark.[19]

Arthur, in fact, had a high priority for seeing Peachtree Street's pristine elegance protected from urban blight. He provided the largest single gift needed to purchase the old Erlanger Theater. It was transformed into a building designed for use by nonprofits and North Avenue Presbyterian Church's outreach programs. The act was part of a coordinated effort to supply anchors for the area extending up to and including Atlanta's Midtown. In Arthur's mind there was much to be preserved in the stretch that includes a historic church—St. Luke's Episcopal—and the Fox and Crawford Long Hospital.[20]

His interest in sports, at all levels, has continued. In 1972 he started Road Atlanta, so as to "bring to NASCAR country the best road racing at the only finished first class track in the Southeast." His service with SunTrust continues, as does his loyalty to University of Georgia sports.[21]

Forward Atlanta

The 1961 Forward Atlanta campaign was the second incarnation of a national advertising blitz first used in the 1920s to attract new businesses to the region. A spate of favorable articles in major media outlets portrayed the "City to Busy to Hate" as moderate in racial attitudes and policies and possessing a pro-business environment. Also spotlighted were Atlanta's position as a regional transportation center and the city's beautiful homes and neighborhoods. While the 1920s program bore the imprint of Ivan Allen Sr., the 1960s promotion was inspired and implemented by Mayor Ivan Allen Jr., both former heads of the Atlanta Chamber of Commerce. The structure and objectives of Atlanta's drive for major league status was actually the six-point platform of Ivan Allen Jr. in his 1961 mayoral campaign. (The six points also were his program for progress when he served as chamber president.) The success with which his platform provisions met across America—and even internationally—shaped present-day Atlanta as "The World's Next Great City." As outlined in a publication of the Atlanta History Cen-ter, the six points that defined the modern-day metro-politan area were: (1) the speeding up of expressway construction; (2) increased urban renewal; (3) the construction of a new civic center and stadium; (4) development of a rapid transit system; (5) a continued plan of gradual but steady school desegregation; and (6) a call for additional low-income housing. In much of this program, the second in Allen's corner was Arthur Montgomery. He was in charge of building a major-league stadium and an arena and bringing in big league baseball and basketball. He also had duties in attracting new businesses—Fortune 500 companies flocked to the city—and in determining the advertising thrust. Did Montgomery and the other leaders succeed? An assessment came in 1980 from Allen himself: "The '60s were the right time. Atlanta was the right city and this business community was the right one. No city has ever seen anything like it before and no city is likely to see it again."[22]

A FASCINATING PANORAMA OF "HIS TERRITORY'S" progress since its days as a small rail terminus graces the Atlanta History Museum at the Atlanta History Center. An article in the Center's quarterly publication, *Atlanta History: A Journal of Georgia and the South*, describes the impressive presentation: "When visitors enter...they are greeted by a glass wall upon which are suspended a number of video monitors. On the other side of the wall, the entire story of Atlanta is arrayed before them, sanctioned off by doors leading to the four period cities. A recording explains how the exhibit is arranged, invites them to "enter history" through the door of their choice, and tells some of the connections between Atlanta's past and present. The introduction shows visitors images of Atlanta's rural life and in the present day, its roots and realities as a modern transportation center, its continuing success as a commercial city, and its unique character as a highly [urbanized and] suburbanized environment."[23]

It seems fair to point out that Arthur Montgomery and his family—since the awarding of the second Coca-Cola bottling franchise in 1900—have played a major part in the dramatic progress of this town that arose, like the phoenix, from the ashes of war in the last century. The display prompts the thought, among some who know him best, that Arthur has made a measure of this unparalleled progress possible.

Arthur "still goes to the office every day" and the returns on his investments in corporate and personal citizenship continue to bear dividends. Those investments have endured, and the increase from them have been enjoyed by his community and his neighbors. They will be drawing interest for a very long time.

Endnotes

[1] Pat Watters, *Coca-Cola: An Illustrated History* (Garden City NY: Doubleday & Co., 1978) 80.

[2] Furman Bisher, *Miracle in Atlanta* (Cleveland OH: World Publishing Co., 1966) 27–28.

[3] James Wimberly, interview by author, Atlanta, Georgia, 30 May 1995.

[4] The Coca-Cola Company Archives, Atlanta, Georgia.

[5] Arthur L. Montgomery biography file, Hargrett Rare Book and Manuscript Collection, University of Georgia Library, Athens, Georgia.

[6] Bill Diehl, "Arthur Montgomery: The Big League Pitch," *The Georgia Alumni Record*, October 1964, 3–6.

[7] Jerry Imlay, interview by author, Atlanta, Georgia, 30 May 1995; William Hartman, interview with author, Athens, Georgia, 11 February 1998.

[8] Ovid R. Davis, conversation with author, Atlanta, Georgia, ca. 1961.

[9] Wimberly interview; letter from Arthur L. Montgomery to Robert W. Woodruff, 19 September 1963, Robert W. Woodruff Collection, Emory University Library, Atlanta, Georgia.

[10] Pat Watters, 81; "Purity Lives in a House of Glass" pamphlet, The Coca-Cola Company, 1954.

[11] Arthur L. Montgomery, interview by author, Atlanta, Georgia, 10 June 1998; Lafayette Montgomery biography, The Coca-Cola Company Archives.

[12] Walter G. Cooper, *The Story of Georgia* (New York: The American Historical Society, 1938) 550; *The Coca-Cola Bottler*, August 1951.

[13] Arthur L. Montgomery, interview by author, Atlanta, Georgia, 10 November 1997.

[14] Ivan Allen Jr., letter to the author, 7 August 1997; Eugene Patterson, "The Big Three: They Created the Stadium in a Uniquely

Southern Way," *Atlanta Journal-Constitution Sunday Magazine*, 4 April 1965, 5.

[15] Norman Shavin, "Plenty of Names, And, Yet, Not One," *Atlanta Constitution*, 1965.

[16] Al Thomy, "A Doer: Montgomery Man in a Hurry," *Atlanta Constitution*, 1970; Murray Olderman, "Between You 'N Me," Newspaper Enterprise Association, 19 November 1964; Morris McLemore, "Battle of Atlanta to Leave Scars for Many Years," *Miami News*, 9 June 1964.

[17] Montgomery interview, 10 June 1998; Jesse Outlar, "Politics Rule Stadium Choice, Not Experience," *Atlanta Constitution*, 10 June 1979; Furman Bisher, "Joker's Wild," *Atlanta Journal*, 23 August 1979.

[18] James B. Williams, interview by author, Atlanta, Georgia, 19 August 1997.

[19] Sales and Marketing Executives-Atlanta, membership bulletin, May 1965; Charley Roberts, *Footballetter*, National Football Foundation Hall of Fame, June-July 1967; University of Georgia College of Veterinary Medicine, news release, 7 April 1994; The Coca-Cola Company Archives; *Atlanta* magazine, May 1976.

[20] Billie Cheney Speed, *Atlanta Journal*, 23 May 1972, A6.

[21] Leslie Savage, seminar paper, Emory University, 18 August 1976.

[22] Ivan Earnest Allen, *Atlanta from the Ashes* (Atlanta: Ruralist Press, 1928) and Darlene R. Roth and Andy Ambrose, *Metropolitan Frontiers: A Short History of Atlanta* (Atlanta: Longstreet Press, 1996).

[23] Darlene R. Roth, "Metropolitan Frontiers," *Atlanta History: A Journal of Georgia and the South* 37 (Fall 1993) 25.

4

THE BARRON FAMILY
OF ROME

Stories about the Barron family—F. S. Barron, his sons Willie and Alfred, and their sons, Frank, Mike, and Al—still circulate both in the soft drink industry and in their former territory based in the Northwest Georgia stronghold of Rome. At various times the family's Rome and Cartersville bottling operations boasted the nation's top per-capita consumption for Coca-Cola, and all of the Barrons were community and industry leaders. Sums up Frank Barron of his family's high order of citizenship and their devotion to the hometown, their territory: "We were the town, and the town was us."[1]

It was William F. Barron, best known as "Mr. Willie," who epitomized the family's great contributions to the industry and their communities. Daily he would wear a black bow tie, just like the ones sported by his route salesmen as they made their rounds. It was he who was the apotheosis of the onetime Coca-Cola advertising tagline, "your friendly, hometown bottler of Coca-Cola."

Willie and his brother, Alfred, assiduously cultivated the territory for the drink first bottled and distributed by their father in 1901, the year after the awarding of the Atlanta franchise and just two years after the initial bottling rights were obtained by George W. Thomas and Joseph B. Whitehead in Chattanooga.[2] Although the franchise was sold to Coca-Cola Company interests in 1986, the memories of Willie's commitment to the community remain. A little league coach will remember how when approaching Mr. Willie about getting new uniforms, the bottler would reach for his checkbook, asking only, "How much you need, coach?" Another former Roman will recall how Willie Barron got him a job in Atlanta so he could pay his way through law school. And an editorial appearing after his death in 1977 in the Rome daily cited his willingness to "extend a helping hand to others" and how he "provided sage counsel or tendered leadership to faltering causes" in the public interest.[3]

All this was part of the tradition begun by F. S. Barron, Willie's father, at the turn of the century. Upon the pioneer's death in 1935, the Rome Rotary Club memorialized F. S. Barron by resolving, "Like some Greatheart of the... mountains, he was 'diligent in business, fervent in spirit, serving the Lord.'" The resolution declared as well, "He applied the principles of Rotary to daily living, placing service above self in all of life's relationships."[4]

F. S.'s children carried on the tradition, taking the lead in numerous positions of community leadership. Willie was president of the Kiwanis. Alfred was a member of the Shorter College board, president of Rotary, and chairman of the local housing authority. Willie served as a key player with the National City Bank. Alfred was a mainstay of the Trust Company of Georgia associate bank, the First National, at the other end of Rome's Broad Street. When Willie backed one leading candidate for governor, Alfred typically would take the lead in supporting the other.[5]

Dignified and tall, crowned by a fine head of red hair and of distinguished mien, Alfred commanded respect for his hard-driving management style and finely honed intellect. He and Willie were formidable competitors and dedicated completely to the economic progress of the region. Their styles differed, but in the results they strove for they were as one.

IN 1901, THE YEAR F. S. BARRON STARTED IN THE SOFT drink business, a revolution was beginning in the turpentine industry. Cotton textile plants were popping up all over the state, and by 1927 Macon's Bibb Manufacturing Company was "the largest cotton mill unit in America" and the second-largest in the world. The Coca-Cola business was going just as well. By 1910 F. S. Barron—now in the upper ranks of civic leadership—joined with four others and Martha Berry of the Berry Schools to bring former President Theodore Roosevelt to the city, where some 15,000 witnessed Teddy perched on a platform made from forty-six bales of Floyd County cotton. Through the years, the ties between the Barrons and the Berry Schools have remained strong; with the success of the Rome bottler, so has come the success of many of their local beneficiaries.[6]

The human side to the Rome Coca-Cola Bottling Company's success continued with F. S.'s son Willie. In 1946 the local high school's splendid new stadium was named Barron Field in his honor, and in 1949 he was named Rome's citizen of the year. In 1964 the high school bands saluted Rome Coca-Cola Bottling Company for their humanitarian contributions to the people of Rome, spelling out the word "Coke" while serenading a crowd of 7,000 to the strains of "Things Go Better with Coke."[7]

In 1962 Coca-Cola Company Chairman Lee Talley took copy prepared by a former Roman on his staff and recorded a tribute to Mr. Willie and his organization. When Barron was scheduled to visit with the chairman, Talley would contact this young copywriter to ask what significant projects he was working on. The reason? "When Willie comes to see me, he always wants to know all the good things his 'Rome boy' is doing." Mr. Willie always was one to champion hometown products, including the young people produced there.[8]

It was typical of Willie Barron that a Rome-area craftsman was the installer of Rome-grown hardwood paneling in the boardroom of the Coca-Cola Bottlers Association, which he headed in 1952–53. Asks Jerry Imlay, a longtime official with the association, to a visitor of the group's Atlanta headquarters, "Isn't it a beautiful reminder of the legacy of Mr. Willie?"[9]

Talley spoke of "a hard-working leader with his familiar black bow tie rising six days each week at 5:30 A.M. to send off his Coca-Cola trucks at 7:00 A.M." and of an institution beloved of its customers, one with "a philosophy of excellence and a creed of service." Duty called Willie to the Coca-Cola business six days a week, but on Sundays he sung a joyful song to the Lord. After the service, though, there always was plenty of Willie's drink for friends and family at the Barron home.[10]

Local businesses were accorded special status as neighbors and customers; all bottling plant purchases went through them as a matter of course. It was at locations like Drummond's River Street Texaco station that many of the plant's several hundred trucks were lined up waiting on

Friday afternoons. Mr. Willie gassed up his vehicles only with the locals, rather than in bulk and at a lower price from an out-of-towner. This loyalty to the Rome business community was a part of the Barron 'creed of service' that Lee Talley so admired.[11]

Three of the Barrons served as presidents of the Rome-Floyd Chamber of Commerce. Willie and son Frank were chairmen of the Georgia Chamber of Commerce, the state's premier industry recruitment organization. Along with Alfred Barron, they led drives attracting large manufacturing plants, such as General Electric, Georgia Kraft, and Bekaert, to Rome. Their town became a major regional industrial center as the newcomers joined the ranks of Pepperell, Brighton, and Celanese. Together they produced a steady stream of income and prosperity with their payrolls. Of course, their workers would get thirsty on the job, as were their families at home. Needless to say, Rome Coca-Cola Bottling, with its ninety to ninety-five percent share of the local market, had just the beverage to quench the community's thirst.[12]

IN 1976 CHARLES MANSON AND HIS "FAMILY" MARKED Willie Barron for execution, one of three "capitalistic pigs" selected in Georgia as part of a much-larger list of business leaders from all over the nation. (The Georgians included a Westinghouse executive in Atlanta and a South Georgia newspaper publisher.) Willie's son Frank, by then prominent in his own right, actually may have been the intended target. The Manson documents, uncovered in one of the houses occupied by the murderers, read only "W. F. Barron," which could have been either father or son—no "senior" or "junior" had been designated on the bizarre hit list.[13]

But why was "W. F. Barron," a bottler in a mid-sized Georgia city, singled out, when neither Robert W. Woodruff or Lee Talley, say, accorded such dubious recognition? It might have been that the Manson Family members had hastily thrown together the hit list and didn't know a Coca-Cola Company executive from one of a thousand Coca-Cola franchise holders. Yet, ironically, Manson managed to single out perhaps the most beloved and respected man in the entire Coca-Cola system.

At any rate, a year or so later, in October 1977, Willie Barron was dead—of natural causes. They blocked off traffic on the main thoroughfares of Rome for the funeral at the packed sanctuary at First Baptist Church. Mourners had to make their way up the hill past the Masonic Temple and past the post office to Willie's church. The familiar clock tower, the city's longtime symbol, looked down on Rome's first citizen and the multitudes of those who loved him.

Frank Barron says—and no one would dispute the statement—"My Daddy was probably the most respected Coca-Cola man in the country, certainly one of the two or three most admired."[14] And he had died in the seventy-fifth year of his franchise's operation. Born in 1898, he thought he had seen it all. But had he? Some radical factors were troubling bottlers around the country. And the Barron family was not immune, as Frank explained to this writer in a narrative expanding on all facets of life in the bottling business, from his earliest memories of it in the mid-1930s up until the 1986 sale of the franchise.

Brought to You by Coca-Cola

In the 1970s, the Coca-Cola Bottlers of Georgia—along with The Coca-Cola Company—underwrote the costs of broadcasting the Vince Dooley Georgia Bulldog Show on a statewide radio hookup reaching all 159 of the state's counties. The show featured the University of Georgia's popular head football coach, a mentor taking his charges to postseason bowl games with great frequency. It was no small undertaking, and Frank Barron played an active part with the aid of the university athletic association's Loran Smith. ("A wonderful man" to work with, Barron remembers.) And these same bottlers supplied free product for the Department of Industry, Trade, and Tourism's welcome stations on the state's borders. After all, the rationale went, Coca-Cola *is* our state's best-known and most admired product. Trouble was, as Georgia succeeded in positioning itself as a prime tourism state, these wel-come stations experienced exceptionally heavy volume—amounting to a powerful lot of sampling and consequently a ton of donated product.[15]

THE STATE OF GEORGIA IN THE FIRST HALF OF THE nineteenth century was a small place. One knew his customers, his fellow bottlers, and the investors in his business. Quite well, in most cases. But in the case of F. S. Barron there was a certain amount of self-generated pressure, for he had "gone broke" twice in the grocery business. Still, the Luptons and the Whiteheads had determined that F. S. was good bottler material, and they awarded him the Rome franchise. The asking price was $250, according to Frank Barron, with Lupton and Whitehead taking five percent in stock and expecting regular dividends. At that time, in 1901, there were only nine bottlers around, and two were in Georgia.[16]

"The Barron territory" was expanding rapidly by the time F. S.'s son Willie returned from World War I. After Rome came Cartersville and then Carrolton, Cedartown, Dalton, Fort Valley, and Valdosta. From the time he was twelve, Willie's son Frank worked at the plant. His first job was sorting bottles; four hours work at twelve and a half cents per hour, or fifty cents a day. Barron describes "working the pocket," driving a slow route truck over unimproved roads—which is to say unpaved, dusty, and hot as the dickens on summer days. He'll tell you about sardine-and-soda-cracker "gourmet" lunches consumed with a Coke from a general store at the crossroads while seated beneath the nearest shade tree. Like all the Barron men, Frank was up at 5:30 A.M. and in to the plant to see the trucks off at 7:00 A.M., six days a week. Everybody in Rome knew the family was made up of early risers who worked for every nickel the customer placed across a counter.[17]

The heart of their thriving enterprise was Rome's Broad Street. When Frank Barron speaks of the place his eyes sparkle (some who grew up with him always thought Frank closely resembled "the Sprite," the elf-like figure with the cheerful smile and sparkling eyes used for so long in Coca-Cola advertising) as he remembers how vibrant it once was. "You saw everybody you knew on that street, and we worked every single store on it," he says, noting that the stores were owned and operated by locals. The Huffman-Salmon grocery was such an active outlet for Coke, he remembers, that on a

Saturday the plant would have to service the store three times.[18]

Fred Coulter, he recalls, was the route salesman who worked Broad Street for nearly forty years. "He was a little, rooster sort of fellow, very attractive personality; everybody knew him and he knew everybody. Man, could he sell Coca-Cola." Coulter's outgoing personality provided entertainment of a sort, as well. Frank recalls the salesman's practice of "whistlin' up the truck" on Rome's main street. It goes something like this: "He had the truck so that if you put it in a certain gear it would move very slowly; but it would move without him." When the absent driver finished servicing one outlet, he would "whistle up" his double-parked truck and it would follow him to the next store. Out-of-towners would gawk in amazement while the Broad Street regulars would chuckle appreciatively of their faithful Coca-Cola man. It was hard to dislike a business run by people like that, they thought.[19]

While there was that very human side to the Barrons and their business, make no mistake that their goal was saturation. Stan Henderson, former owner of an outdoor advertising company in the Barron territory, states that he never had to come groveling to them for a little business. "Heck, no" says Henderson. "Before I could hardly get the legs of a new board in the ground, here would come a call from Mr. Barron." Without even identifying himself, Barron would say, "I want that one, too!"[20] Universality of distribution? Yes, the product was available at every possible outlet, and the trademark was on every possible advertising medium, stimulating demand. The Barrons were 100 percenters at this business and it showed. They also were all-out for whatever was good for their hometown—and for the other cities in their territory.

AS AN ADULT, FRANK BARRON WAS NEVER ANY-thing but "a Coca-Cola man," from the time he went to work after returning from service in the U.S. Navy in 1956 until the sale of the business thirty years later in 1986. (He remains a consultant to and representative of The Coca-Cola Company.) In a 1982 interview, Frank Barron spoke of the lines of work he had been involved with during his career. "The first work I ever recall doing, I was about twelve...sorting bottles, separating them before they were washed. I've fixed coolers and delivered coolers, filled the washers with empty bottles, washed trucks, kept books—we all have. There's nothing I haven't done in this operation except be a sign painter. But I've helped erect signs. My son has painted signs. That's one thing he's done that I haven't done!"[21]

Frank once told a writer doing an article for a Berry College publication, "About work? I have a ball. I'd rather be the 'Coca-Cola man' than Santa Claus." He adds, "At least in Rome, Georgia, you can be the 'Coca-Cola man' 365 days a year, but you can be Santa Claus only once a year." The part of his job Frank relished was involvement in worthwhile causes. A look at his resume reveals that: chairman and president, Georgia Chamber of Commerce; trustee, Berry College; trustee, Darlington School; president, Georgia Baptist Foundation. The list extends over another page, single-spaced. On it goes, lifetime trustee of the governing body for the Carter Presidential Center in Atlanta, board member of the National Soft Drink Association.[22]

The Barron family excelled at dividing the duties and responsibilities so that each could make a distinct contribution to the enterprise. After Willie's death his brother Alfred had responsibility for the Rome operation. Frank ran Dalton and Cartersville; Mike ran Valdosta and Carrolton; and Al ran Fort Valley and Cedartown. All of them worked as hard and long as they ever had, although shortly before Willie's death Alfred had persuaded his older brother that it was no longer necessary to work a six-day week. It was in matters such as the work week that Frank concedes that Alfred and Willie could be rather recalcitrant concerning change. Frank Barron even describes them as paternalistic; "they kind of knew what was best for everybody."[23]

For one thing, they felt it was almost a sin to change a route around, maintaining that their customers depended on their men working the same runs. Another objection was to cutting back on weekly deliveries in order to give more attention to the mushrooming chain operations. A chain's buyer, Frank and other Coca-Cola bottlers ruefully discovered, could make your life miserable with constant demands and burdensome house rules—requests to discount the product and quit expensive network television advertising. In the 1970s Kroger even sent word that they didn't care to negotiate with the scores of bottlers throughout Georgia—most of them with varying wholesale prices. They insisted that the staff man for the Council of Coca-Cola Bottlers of Georgia just bring them one price for the huge quantity of product to be "specialed" at a discount price for shoppers. Bottlers had little choice but to acquiesce to the grocery store chain.[24]

As the pace picked up for bottlers of all kinds, everywhere, it bewildered businessmen who knew hometown accounts intimately and who had resisted for years the breaking of the nickel retail price barrier and the six-and-one-half-ounce bottle. By 1956, a second container size, the ten ounce, was added. Product lines diversified and distribution expanded. Soon cans and non-returnable containers edged out the returnable bottle. Frank Barron points out that while some might take him to task for the environmentally unfriendly "throwaways," he explains that it was the customer who brought that about, people who'd pay a deposit and then "just drive down the road and throw that bottle of mine away."[25]

Along with all the change came a 1965 initiative of Coca-Cola Company CEO J. Paul Austin: special, high-level training for the bottlers at Harvard University's School of Business. Harvard, as most of the "students" were aware, was the alma mater of the chief executive. "Paul was president, and he thought that the average Coca-Cola bottler was woefully uneducated — and he was right," concedes Barron. About thirty-two or thirty-three years of age at the time, Barron took back to his territory and dutifully applied the lessons learned in marketing, money management, and people management. He installed a new inventory control system complete with hand-held computers for his route men.[26]

Another problem at the time revolved around the bottlers cooperative advertising programs, which had become increasingly complex and unwieldy. Advertising costs were allocated among a dozen or more bottlers, giving them the right, they felt, to question the parent company's advertising subjects and themes. "All the older guys would say that the stuff (television ads) was childish or not good; they thought all we needed to say was 'Coca-Cola refreshes.'" (While Barron admits that all the ads were not uniform in their excellence, he asks, "Who couldn't like the 'Mean Joe Greene' commercial or the one of all the kids singing 'I'd like to give the world a Coke'"?)[27]

Meanwhile, in the 1970s a new state-of-the-art bottling plant was built, necessitating the closing of what had become the oldest continuously operating Coca-Cola bottling facility—the plant on North Fifth Avenue across from the courthouse.

As these and other complications multiplied, along came a development that sent shock waves throughout the soft drink industry: a ruling by the Federal Trade Commission striking down "the walls" (in Frank Barron's phrase) of bottlers' protected territories. (The Coca-Cola Company's provision of territories had been a strong incentive for the first bottlers, whose ventures were by no means guaranteed.) At roughly this same time The Coca-Cola Company began to press for "amended contracts" with its bottlers to obtain some protection against a competitor's inroads, such as demanding first right of refusal for families wishing to sell. A battle royal over the "walls down" threat was soon being waged, with Frank Barron playing a major role by virtue of his involvement with the National Soft Drink Association, the powerful voice of the industry. It hurt not at all, some in the industry recall, that those Georgians in the Coca-Cola business were on good terms with President Jimmy Carter, the former Georgia governor. Luckily, says Barron, at this time bottlers were still rather powerful in a political sense; one could just about bet that a given U.S. Representative or Senator would know his home-town Coca-Cola bottler on a first-name basis. Consolidation of territories and a wave of franchise selling, however, diluted that long-cultivated political clout, he says.[28]

With all the change, Barron continued, "this was an industry that was fixing to kill itself." A measure known as

The Intrabrand Competition Act, introduced by Senator Birch Bayh of Indiana, combined with President Carter's support and understanding of the issue to get the bottlers out of the jam. But Barron felt it was just a matter of time until the steamroller of consolidation, aided by Carter's 1980 defeat, would crush the bottlers in its path.[29]

One-Calorie Tab

After some fits and starts amid concern over possible carcinogenic content, there at last emerged an artificial sweetener acceptable to the health and environmental agencies within the Federal establishment. And so in 1964 was launched Tab, The Coca-Cola Company's first "dietetic" soft drink. (Sounded too much like "diabetic," said some bottlers.[30]) Frank Barron himself became a drinker of Tab—"keep Tab of your calories!," you know.

FRANK AND HIS COUSINS AL AND MIKE—WITH UNCLE Alfred in agreement—soon came to the realization that "we were ringed in." What brought things to a head was the Barrons' bid to purchase the Tallahassee, Florida, bottling franchise. It would have rounded out their portfolio quite nicely, but the stakes were simply too high. To the south, Atlanta had been bought by The Company, as had the Lupton interests in Chattanooga to the north. To the west lay the Crawford Johnson Company in Birmingham, an insurmountable object for the Barrons. (The Johnson group now is the third-largest bottling operation in the U.S.) To the east were the Carolinas, the property of Coca-Cola Consolidated, now second-largest among U.S. bottlers. So, the Barrons did what so many were then doing. They sold.[31]

While of course there is logic in this sort of consolidation among the biggest bottlers, a sad side effect to the trend is the absence of "your friendly neighbor who bottles Coca-Cola" from the American main street, neighbors such as Frank Barron. Walking by the old North Fifth Avenue facility, he says, "We took our money and we ran and I guess I don't regret it." Frank continues, "There are days when I regret what it used to be—the old days, the camaraderie, and I miss the people and all that." Then he cannot help but add, "The way it was when we finally sold out was not as much fun as, I guess, it had once been. Perhaps I had gotten older or perhaps I had gotten jaded, but for whatever reason I have never looked back."[32]

A neighbor of Frank's read and reread those words. Shaking his head, he concluded, "No, of course Frank looks back—and looks back with pride on what he and his family were to Rome; I know I do."[33]

Endnotes

[1] *The Coca-Cola Bottler,* November 1935, 28-29; W. Frank Barron, interview by author, Rome, Georgia, 13 January 1994.

[2] Franklin M. Garrett, *The Coca-Cola Company: An Illustrated Profile* (Atlanta: The Coca- Cola Company, 1974) 23-31.

[3] *The Rome News-Tribune,* 6 October 1977, 4.

[4] Resolution, The Rotary Club of Rome, Georgia, adopted 26 September 1935.

[5] Loran Smith, "Barrons Making Sure Rome Folks Still Get the Real Thing," *Athens Daily News/Banner-Herald,* 9 August 1998, F3.

[6] Mary Savage Anderson, *Georgia: A Pageant of Years* (Spartanburg SC: The Reprint Co., 1974); Roger Aycock, *All Roads to Rome* (Roswell GA: W. H. Wolfe Assoc., 1981) 286-91; *Berry Quarterly,* Summer 1982.

[7] *The Coca-Cola Bottler,* December 1963, 31; *Salute to a Bottler* (Atlanta: Hickory Publishing Company, nd).

[8] Recollection of the author, ca. 1960.

[9] Jerry Imlay, interview by the author, Atlanta, Georgia, 30 May 1995.

[10] W. Frank Barron, interview by author, Rome, Georgia, 31 July 1998.

[11] Ibid.

[12] Ibid.

[13] Ibid.

[14] Ibid.

[15] W. Frank Barron and employees of the University of Georgia Athletic Association and the Georgia Department of Industry, Trade, and Tourism, interviews by author, Atlanta, Athens, and Rome, Georgia, 1998.

[16] Aycock, *All Roads to Rome,* 286-291; Hartnett T. Kane with Inez Henry, *Miracle in the Mountains* (New York: Doubleday and Co., 1956) 202-215.

[17] Barron interview.

[18] Ibid.

[19] Ibid.

[20] Stan Henderson, interview by author, Athens, Georgia, 23 July 1998.

[21] W. Frank Barron, speech to Rome Kiwanis Club, 30 July 1962.

[22] Barron interview.

[23] Ibid.

[24] Ibid.

[25] Ibid.

[26] Ibid.

[27] Ibid.

[28] Ibid.

[29] Ibid.; Intrabrand Competition Act of 1978.

[30] Coca-Cola Company/Bottlers Meeting, Houston District, Southwest Region, San Antonio, Texas, Spring 1964

[31] Barron interview; Keith Herndon, "Coke Will Buy $1.4 Billion Worth of Bottling Businesses," *Atlanta Constitution*, 2 July 1986.

[32] Mark Pendergrast, *For God, Country, and Coca-Cola* (New York: Simon and Schuster, 1997) 377–378; Barron interview.

[33] James W. Wimberly, interview by author, Atlanta, Georgia, 22 February 1997.

5

THE ROBERTS FAMILY
OF COLUMBUS

Every time the church doors were opened, he was there,"
recounts Columbus Roberts III about his grandfather.[1] So
perhaps it shouldn't be surprising that Dr. Spright Dowell,
past president of the Baptist-affiliated Mercer University,
wrote an exceptional biography of the grandfather, entitled
Columbus Roberts: Christian Steward Extraordinary.[2]

The Coca-Cola bottler for the Columbus, Georgia, market
was a leading Baptist layman, but his contributions to
business, agriculture, and public service in Georgia were
considerable as well. Civic leadership was a priority, and his
philanthropy—much of it related to the works of his
denomination and its church-related colleges and universi-
ties—was legendary. His family even had to purchase his
grandfather an automobile after he donated virtually all he
owned to charity.[3]

In Dowell's book, the Columbus man is quoted as saying:
"As my sixty-fifth birthday drew near [in 1935], my thoughts
turned toward retirement from business and the assumption of
other duties, which, I felt, were of greater importance." That
would involve devoting "my life to the service of my fellow
men and to the service of God." So, Roberts said, "I gave the

business to my children on December 31, 1935." That meant he could devote more time to public service, eventually becoming Georgia's Secretary of Agriculture on 1 January 1937. He already had served in the Georgia House of Representatives representing Muscogee County and as chairman of the House Agriculture Committee. Service as agriculture commissioner, a position of scarcely less influence than that of Georgia's governor, was capped with a spirited race for the top job itself in 1940.[4]

In a stellar field of candidates, Roberts came close to defeating Eugene Talmadge. And it was a campaign financed totally by Roberts himself, who wished to be free of any taint. "My intent was to win the office...on my own merits, and I did not wish to be beholden to any individual, group, or clique; but only to the people of Georgia." And those who knew the high-minded candidate, whose hallmark was integrity, knew he meant it. Here was a man elected to the agriculture commissioner's position in 1936 embracing Franklin D. Roosevelt's New Deal and "associating myself with a group of liberals who identified themselves with the New Deal by adopting the slogan of 'The Four R's—Roosevelt, Russell, Rivers, and Roberts.'" (The "Russell" referred to was Georgia's U.S. Senator Richard B. Russell; and the "Rivers" was Georgia Governor E. D. Rivers.)[5]

There were many in his day who regarded Columbus Roberts only as a political figure. Others saw him as a dedicated man of God who endowed Mercer University with the equivalent of $22 million in 1997 dollars. (And this does not include gifts to several other Baptist schools, such as Bessie Tift College.) A great many other Georgians realized him to be both of these things, as well as a phenomenally successful businessman. Only a very few realized Roberts, the self-made man, had received only four years of formal education (although he freely acknowledged as much to Spright Dowell in his biography).[6]

Building a Better Farm

Thirty miles from Columbus, in Warm Springs, President Franklin Delano Roosevelt had a showplace of a demonstration farm with 2,700 acres. Also in Harris County was the highly publicized Pine Mountain Valley Community, a cooperative experiment launched with great support from the president, who often visited and helped tout the effort. Nearby was Blue Springs, a farm owned and developed by textile-magnate-turned-farmer Cason J. Callaway, a confidant of and frequent visitor of Roosevelt. The farm later became the site of Callaway Gardens, a Garden of Eden grown out of the worn and undernourished soil of West Georgia. Along with his efforts at Blue Springs, Callaway initiated an ambitious "One Hundred Better Georgia Farms" program, designed to attract businesses dedicated to scientific farming. In this initiative, Callaway—a board member of The Coca-Cola Company and the first Southerner ever named to the board of U.S. Steel—had the cooperation of a number of Coca-Cola people, many of whom were in-volved in farming themselves.[7]

IN THE SUMMER OF 1900, IN OPELIKA, ALABAMA, Joseph B. Whitehead, general manager of his and J. T. Lupton's Coca-Cola Bottling Company, was making one of his many calls upon promising men of the South. His goal was to interest them in buying into the Coca-Cola business.[8]

One of the men to whom Whitehead made his pitch was Columbus Roberts, a Beulah, Alabama, native and one of ten children of a tenant farmer. Just thirty years old, Roberts had already made his mark in the grocery business and as a soft drink bottler (though not of Coca-Cola). Roberts replied to Whitehead, "Give me some time to think it over."[9]

In the meantime, Roberts was conducting his own marketing poll, surveying his customers at every opportunity. The verdict was that Coca-Cola was becoming immensely popular. He "arrived at the conclusion that Coca-Cola might become half of the soft drink business, and that whoever bottled it might also have the opportunity to take over the other half." After thinking it over, Roberts signed a franchise contract in 1901; his firm became the third to be awarded a bottling contract in Georgia. (The operation is now owned by Coca-Cola United out of Birmingham, having been sold for the first time in 1970 to a Dallas company.)

The new firm had a territory including Columbus, Richland, Manchester, LaGrange, and West Point in Georgia, and Opelika, Tuskegee, La Fayette, Dadeville, Hurtsboro, Eufaula, and Alexander City in Alabama. Curtis Roberts, Columbus Roberts's brother, was to run the Columbus plant and Columbus was to run the Opelika operation. (Brother-in-law Dr. Jesse Miller ran the Alexander City plant; another brother-in-law, George C. Cobb, later bought LaGrange and West Point.) After the runaway success of the business in Columbus, Roberts traded places with brother Curtis and began to run things in the Muscogee county seat.[10]

One of the first things Columbus Roberts did was to pay a consultant $2,500 to analyze the business. What the expert "drilled into me was the value, indeed the necessity, of the end-of-the-month inventory." (Apparently, few small town business folks of that day knew much about such a process or fewer thought about installing it.) Dowell quotes him as saying "after studying my periodical inventories, I could tell where my weaknesses and my strengths were." Too, he knew "the operational cost of each department, supplies on hand, supplies ordered, and supplies needed." While Roberts obviously recognized the role the consultant played in his business success, he also credited much of that success to his deep faith:

> I frequently said that whenever the Lord gave me the money to buy a lot, I was going to build a plant of my own. When the 1903 season closed, I found that I had a surplus of $15,000 in the bank. With this I bought the lot I wanted...I humbly regarded my success as an evidence of divine sanction and divine leadership. In this belief, my faith is unshakable, not be it remembered, because I was anything more than a humble servant, but because I felt there was a divine purpose that one day would be revealed.[11]

Like the servant Jesus Christ spoke of in Matthew 25, Roberts took the talent and made a return to the master many times over that of the original gift. The product he bottled, distributed, and sold was becoming America's favorite beverage, and universal distribution and memorable advertising was taking it to yet another level of success. He later would state that the years between 1902, when he made the fateful decision to accept the franchise, and 1920 were the most productive of his life.[12]

The bottling industry pioneer was one to pay attention to detail. Perhaps before many others in his business came to grips with a common problem, he found ways to "secure prompter return of empty bottles" and "reduce the cost of transportation." The investment in the "glass," in industry parlance, was a critical factor in any bottler's success, and Roberts discovered means of keeping the returnable containers in motion. The bottles were in constant use, with some getting as many as one hundred trips to the consumer.[13]

Chief among the factors behind the success in his bottling operation, he concedes, may have been the fact that with World War I raging in Europe "business in America began to experience a great expansion."[14] For him, a dramatic compounding of that prosperity came as the giant Fort Benning Army training facility was established in Columbus. "I had seen to it every canteen in the great cantonment was fully supplied with Coca-Cola," Roberts said, and "it was as though a great city had gratuitously been added to my territory."[15] Sales in the Fort Benning-Columbus area experienced another dramatic upturn with America's entry into World War II.

In addition to bottling, Roberts had expanded into other important and successful ventures. Among them: a hotel, an automobile agency, and a sizable (988 acres) dairying and farming operation. He was a leading raiser of registered Jersey cattle, forming and presiding over the Georgia Milk Producers Confederation. Later on he became head of the state milk board, working tirelessly for price supports for the Georgia dairyman.[16]

"I made it a point to be in my place in church on Sundays and to take an active role in the affairs of my community," he wrote. But, also, "I strove to align myself with those citizens of

Columbus and of Georgia who were definitely committed to the upbuilding of the city and of the great commonwealth." Such a civic leader was William Clark Bradley, the leading planter, banker, industrialist, and businessman of his day in the Muscogee County river port and textile center. For twenty-seven years, from 1919 to 1946, Bradley was chairman of the board of The Coca-Cola Company. Importantly, he was also the mentor of Robert W. Woodruff—the absolute monarch of the Coca-Cola empire worldwide for well over six decades.[17]

Roberts became president of both the state and hometown YMCAs, as well as the local Kiwanis Club. He was a member of the city's water board and president of the Chattahoochee Valley Fair Association, as well as the Chattahoochee Motor Club. And, of course, he was a deacon at the First Baptist Church and chairman of the Georgia Baptist Convention's holding commission. It was through the holding commission that Roberts became acquainted with the perilous financial situation facing Mercer University; he would soon help to rescue the Baptist institution.[18]

With all that he provided in civic, community, and religious leadership, the man from Columbus was faithful to the discharge of his duties in the bottling business. Roberts turned the reins over to son Columbus Roberts Jr. in 1931, and died a month short of age eighty in 1950. But he had provided a sound foundation and uncommon leadership not only to his business but to almost every worthy endeavor in his home city. His influence was felt in the highest councils of those organizations benefiting Georgia and Georgians most.[19]

In any assessment, Columbus Roberts gave thanks to his maker in words like these: "My objective during those years was... to build a worthy business on a secure foundation. For the handicaps He assisted me to overcome through the help of my devoted wife and other loyal friends; and for the triumphs which He enabled me to achieve, I thank God."[20]

In 1929, the people of Muscogee County sent Columbus Roberts to the Georgia General Assembly for a term in the House of Representatives. They returned him to that post in 1931, and he became chairman of the powerful House Committee on Agriculture. It seemed a natural choice for his colleagues and Governor Richard B. Russell to make, for at this point in his career Roberts was heavily involved in farming and dairying. In 1934, with President Roosevelt's "New Deal" for agriculture and the farmers' and FDR's concern for the South as "one-third of a nation ill-clad and ill-fed," Roberts had his work cut out for him when he announced his candidacy for the post of Georgia Secretary of Agriculture.[21] While his first campaign fell short of victory, in 1936, with Roosevelt's support, Roberts won the seat.

Roberts's reform of and administrative work in the Georgia Department of Agriculture won high marks. And in pursuit of his duties, the secretary was a model of rectitude and efficiency. Roberts's style was in marked contrast to the highly politicized office run by "The Wild Man of Sugar Creek," Eugene Talmadge, a former holder of the office and a renowned campaigner—as well as being a friend of the little people in Georgia, who were his rural neighbors and devoted followers. The man with the trademark red galluses and defiant forelock was elected to the governorship three times. Veteran observers of the state's political scene say that Talmadge's campaign rallies were high theater of a rustic nature, providing entertainment, barbecue, and excitement to many a Talmadge partisan on a summer afternoon on the courthouse square.[22]

However, the man who succeeded "Ol' Gene" after his first term in 1932 was Eurith D. Rivers. Like Talmadge, Rivers was a flamboyant campaigner and stem-winding orator, but that's where the similarities ended. In 1934 Rivers called for "A Little New Deal for Georgia." In Roberts's second try for the agriculture job—this time for a four-year term—he proudly became a part of a ticket appealing to the voters of Depression-era Georgia: Roosevelt, Russell, Rivers, and Roberts. (Until his death in 1946, Talmadge would take up the cudgel in opposition to the policies—and these four principals—of the New Deal in Georgia.)[23]

In 1940, Roberts squared off in a three-way, self-financed race for chief executive with Gene Talmadge and prominent Athens attorney Abit Nix. In such a field, Gene resorted to a familiar tactic picturing the pair of opponents as being representative of "the better element." (This came in a year when a majority of Georgia farmers were earning less than $600 a year working the soil.) What is most worthy of note about that contest is not the anti-Roosevelt or pro-New deal rhetoric, but Columbus Roberts's spotless record and the high moral tone in his campaign. In an editorial after his death in 1950, the *Columbus Ledger* noted the "state would have done well to elect him, but as happens in politics the best man often loses to the best politician."[24]

What his fellow Coca-Cola bottlers and his Columbus admirers recall is what Roberts was able to accomplish in the agriculture job and during his legislative service. Columbus Roberts III relates that even today, more than a half century after the race for the governorship, old timers or close observers of the political scene will declare that Roberts should have won the prize. As an elderly African American acquaintance once expressed to Columbus Roberts III, "If the black folks could have voted back then, your granddaddy would've been governor of Georgia."[25]

Columbus Roberts was proud of his "record for economy and efficiency" as the Georgia Agriculture Commissioner. He turned in a sizable surplus upon leaving office and restored *The Farmers Market Bulletin*—issued by the state department of agriculture and distributed free to thousands of Georgia's rural populace—to its original role as a mouthpiece for the farmer. (Roberts believed the newspaper had become "a propaganda sheet" used for "political ends" under the authority of his predecessor, Tom Linder.) As a candidate for governor, he vowed to fight even harder—battling charges of illegal contract negotiations in the highway department and striving for rural electrification. Roberts also had the courage to take on reform of the state's County Unit System, a policy under which all of Georgia's 159 counties carried equal weight as "units," regardless of each county's total population. It was not until 1962, in the case of *Baker v. Carr*, when the courts struck down the system, insisting on a "one man, one vote" criterion, or election solely by popular vote.[26] But while Columbus Roberts lost his bid for the governorship, the understated Roberts ("I was not a skilled campaigner") won the respect of Georgians who appreciated the man's sincerity, ability, and foresight.[27]

Following his failed campaign for governor, the seventy-year-old Roberts set out to find yet another avenue of service. "I would build a city upon a hill, a city of light," he decided, and the "city of light to which I lifted up my eyes was none other than Mercer University." He left his mark on the institution in dozens of ways, including a building for the newly created Roberts School of Religion. In his biography of the bottler, Spright Dowell states that what Jesse Mercer was to its first century, Columbus Roberts was to its second.[28]

With Roberts's help, Mercer would be able to help "furnish a thoroughly trained and well-equipped ministry," the standard sought by Southern Baptist Seminary President E. Y. Mullins and others prominent in leadership circles of the Southern Baptist denomination. Mercer president Spright Dowell constantly advocated the same.[29] Such a well-educated ministry was not always a top priority for Baptist congregations, writes O. K. Armstrong in *The Indomitable Baptists.* For decades, says the author, "many Baptists feared education would wean the preacher away from heartfelt religion." But sometime in the nineteenth century "worshipers turned away from a desire to hear an emotional harangue and favored more thoughtful, well-ordered sermons."

When Mullins took office at Louisville in 1899, "only half of the student body had bachelor degrees, with some even lacking a high school diploma." But for the last several decades Baptist seminaries have required a bachelor's degree from an accredited college, in great part due to the philanthropy and leadership of those of the same mind as Columbus Roberts. Roberts noted, as well, that in his experience when a church had educated leadership, problems and dissension were fewer. Of this, no doubt, he had been persuaded by Dowell and Mullins.[30]

Upon Roberts's death, Dr. C. DeWitt Matthews, a columnist for *The Macon Telegraph* and a pastor at Vineville Baptist Church, wrote that Roberts's total philanthropy was more than $2.5 million. (In current dollars the amount would be in the $55 million range.) Almost half the total went to Mercer, but there were other collegiate beneficiaries in

Georgia with Baptist connections: Bessie Tift, Shorter, Brewton-Parker, Norman Junior, and Truett-McConnell.

Matthews remembered in a column shortly after Roberts's death how unassuming the Coca-Cola man was, how simply he lived; the point often was made by others who knew him as well. Jim Wimberly is a retired vice president for The Coca-Cola Company in Atlanta whose responsibilities included bottler sales in Georgia and the Southeast. He remembers, as a young man, how he went with a delegation from the company to Roberts's funeral and paid a visit to the family at the home. The modest residence had linoleum flooring of the same sort that appeared in most of the homes of Georgia farmers of that era.[31]

Columbus Roberts, the great giver, disposed of most of his Coca-Cola-made wealth, keeping only his home and his farm, and arranging for his foundation to pay out $8,000 annually for upkeep. He told Spright Dowell, "I would return God's loan by sharing it with his people." And he explained, "It should go to the young men and women here in Georgia, who needed it for a worthy purpose and whose mothers and fathers I had known and loved."[32] Roberts's experiences in church work gave him an appreciation for the indoctrination young people gained while being educated at places like Mercer, and for the good works they did when they returned back home.

ON THE SUNDAY BEFORE ROBERTS'S DEATH, DR. Dowell looked out to see him in his sanctuary. Afterwards, the educator recalled, Roberts remained seated for a long while "and seemed reluctant to go." But, whatever his thoughts were, he had just weeks earlier provided Matthews, the *Telegraph* columnist, an insightful self-assessment. To what did Roberts owe his considerable success? First, "my religion and a sincere effort to lead a good life all these years." Second, "dogged application to my job and devotion to duty." Third? The "influence of two people above all—that of my mother and an Atlanta business man, whose life, a life of goodness, became my ideal."[33]

Nothing out of character or surprising about any of that. But "an Atlanta business man," who could that have been? Some think it was Coca-Cola Company founder Asa G. Candler himself, who did so much for Methodism and for Emory University. Those so persuaded say Candler furnished the model that Roberts followed.

Claude McBride, a native of Roberts's hometown, is a winner of a Pulitzer prize for journalism and a onetime Baptist minister in several Georgia cites. And he has a theory about what is was the Coca-Cola man pondered there in the pew on his last Sunday on earth. Perhaps, he surmises, "Mr. Roberts was mentally conducting one of his 'inventories.' This one, it may have been, had to do with the account he—like the servant in the parable—would render his master." Concludes McBride, "from everything I know about him, if that were the case, then by that Saturday morning on which he died he surely would have been fully prepared, in Dr. Dowell's words, to 'go home'."[34]

Endnotes

[1] Columbus Roberts III, interview by author, Columbus, Georgia, 6 February 1998.

[2] Spright Dowell, *Columbus Roberts Christian Steward Extraordinary* (Nashville: Broadman, 1951; reprint Macon: Mercer University Press, 1983).

[3] Roberts interview.

[4] Dowell, *Columbus Roberts*, 119–120; Ralph G. Cooper, *The Story of Georgia: Biographical* (Atlanta: The Reprint Company, 1938) 4:76.

[5] Dowell, *Columbus Roberts*, 123–128

[6] Letter from R. Kirby Godsey, president of Mercer University, to the author, 11 August 1997; Dowell, *Columbus Roberts*, 17.

[7] Papers of W. Tapley Bennett Sr., Hargrett Rare Book and Manuscript Library, University of Georgia; Paul Schubert, *Cason Callaway of Blue Springs* (Hamilton GA: privately printed, 1964), 106–111; Michael Anderson, interview by author, Ida Cason Callaway Gardens, 20 May 1998; William W. Winn, "The View from Dowdell's Knob," *The New Georgia Guide* (Athens: University of Georgia Press, 1996); Howard H. Callaway, *The Story of a Man and a Garden: Cason Callaway and Callaway Gardens* (New York: Newcomen Society in North America, 1965) 1-28.

[8] Franklin M. Garrett, *The Coca-Cola Company: An Illustrated Profile* (Atlanta: The Coca-Cola Company, 1974) 83–84; *The Benwood Foundation: The First 50 Years* (Chattanooga: Benwood Foundation, 1995); see also Franklin M. Garrett, "Coca-Cola in Bottles," *The Coca-Cola Bottler*, April 1959, 79–82.

[9] Dowell, *Columbus Roberts*, 62–63.

[10] The Coca-Cola Company Archives, Atlanta, Georgia; Dowell, *Columbus Roberts*, 80.

[11] Dowell, *Columbus Roberts*, 68–69.

[12] Dowell, *Columbus Roberts*, 82–83, 106–116; Cooper, 76.

[13] Dowell, *Columbus Roberts*, 59–60, 70.

[14] William A. Turner, Bradley-Turner Foundation, interview with author, Columbus, Georgia, 26 January 1998.

[15] Cooper, *The Story of Georgia*, 76.

[16] Dowell, *Columbus Roberts*, 84–85.

[17] Cooper, *The Story of Georgia*, 76; Michael S. Holmes, *The New Deal in Georgia* (Westport CT: Greenwood Press, 1975) 274–276.

[18] Dowell, *Columbus Roberts*.

[19] Dowell, *Columbus Roberts*; The Coca-Cola Company Archives; Charles Lee Kiester, "Theoretical Considerations in the Distribution of Coca-Cola Bottling Plants and Warehouses in Georgia" (master's thesis, University of Georgia, 1972) 54.

[20] Dowell, *Columbus Roberts*.

[21] *Georgia's Official Register* (Georgia Department of Archives and History, 1964) 1043; Winn, "The View from Dowdell's Knob," 374–376.

[22] *Georgia's Official Register*, 1043.

[23] Allen Lumpkin Henson, *Red Galluses: A Tale of Georgia Politics* (Boston: House of Edinboro, 1945) 60–65.

[24] Editorial, *Columbus Ledger*, 28 August 1950.

[25] Roberts interview.

[26] *Baker v. Carr*, 369 U.S. 186, 1962.

[27] Dowell, *Columbus Roberts*, 113–117, 124; Henson, 240–243.

[28] O. K. Armstrong, *The Indomitable Baptists* (Garden City NY: Doubleday, 1967) 283–284; William E. Ellis, *A Man of Books and a Man of the People: E. Y. Mullins and the Crisis of Moderate Baptist Leadership* (Macon: Mercer University Press, 1985) 46; Dowell, *Columbus Roberts*, 149–150.

[29] Dowell, *Columbus Roberts*, 134; Ellis, *A Man of Books and a Man of the People*, 41–44.

[30] Dowell, *Columbus Roberts*, 12–14; editorial, *Opelika News*, 28 August 1950, cited in Dowell, *Columbus Roberts*, 162.

[31] C. DeWitt Matthews, "Down this Road," *Macon Telegraph*, 31 August 1950, cited in Dowell, *Columbus Roberts*, 165–167; editorial, *Atlanta Constitution*, 29 August 1950, cited in Dowell, *Columbus Roberts*, 143; James W. Wimberly, interview by author, Atlanta, Georgia, 22 February 1997.

[32] Dowell, *Columbus Roberts*, 147.

[33] Dowell, *Columbus Roberts*, 148–149.

[34] Claude W. McBride, interview by author, Athens, Georgia, 31 May 1998.

6

THE SAMS FAMILY
OF ATHENS

In the second decade of the twentieth century the boll weevil visited its destruction upon King Cotton, the South's preeminent cash crop. It was this pestilential invader from south of the border, according to legend, that drove Walter A. Sams, one of eleven children, from his farm and ancestral home in Fayette County, Georgia.

Sams's first cousin, Fayetteville, Georgia-based physician and author Ferrol Sams, viewed his kinsman's abandonment with contempt — at least if one extrapolates from a supposedly fictional account in Ferrol's first novel, *Run with the Horsemen*. "A cousin had surrendered to the boll weevil," he wrote, "and moved out of the county and bought Coca-Cola stock." Then comes the judgment, "He was rich, but there was the unspoken disdain for him because he left the land." Ferrol Sams, like so many agrarian Southerners of that time, actually felt that "without the land there would be no family."[1]

In fact, Walter Sams was just as devoted as his cousin to family, tradition, and land — he just took a different direction. Sams was a born trader in much the same way as Asa G. Candler and Robert W. Woodruff. Like Candler, he would become a pharmacist, selling and reselling his Marietta shop numerous times, always at a neat profit. In between, he would buy and sell Coca-Cola franchises until, in the words of Coca-Cola Company historian Franklin Garrett, he "finally found one he liked." That one would be in Athens, Georgia.[2]

Once settled in Athens (thanks to the aid of previous Athens bottler C. Veazey Rainwater), Sams reestablished his ties to the land, staking out a large-acreage operation in Clarke County. He would at times close down the bottling plant and take employees to his place to bale hay. "What a character he was," observes Millard Epps, a thirty-four-year veteran of the business. "He even painted numbers on the cows because he wanted to know exactly which one was which." Grandson Walter A. "Corky" Sams III (who ended up running the franchise before its 1985 sale, with first cousin Albert "Buddy" Sams), recalls his grandfather's automobile cow horn. The elder Sams delighted in taking grandkids to the acreage and chasing after the cattle, sounding the horn, and laughing all the while. Though he never made any money on it, Sams adored his farm; it was sold to the University of Georgia School of Agriculture after his death.[3]

It was Otis Landrum who ran the farm for Sams. Recalls Landrum's grandson, Rick Dawson, "Mr. Sams was a dedicated practitioner of modern farming methods in a time when much of our farm land was all but exhausted and abandoned during the Great Depression. It was just about farmed out—eroded and incapable of producing a decent yield." Continues Dawson, "He listened to every idea for improving the soil my granddad offered, and he encouraged the Ag school and soil conservation people to experiment with him in the public interest. I guess you could say he was a kind of visionary, and the present property bears witness to the fact that his dream pretty much came true."[4]

THE UBIQUITOUS EVANGEL OF A POST-RECONSTRUCT-
ion New South was Henry W. Grady, an Athens native and
famed editor of *The Atlanta Constitution*. He encouraged young
Southerners to compete with their counterparts from the North
in the lists of commerce and industry. Mark Twain took note
of this new breed of southerner, calling them "brisk men,
energetic of movement and speech; the dollar their god, how
to get it their religion." Even the fiery populist and U.S.
Senator from Georgia, Tom Watson, exhorted: "Let the young
South arise in their might and compete with the (Yankees) in
everything.... Get rich! If you have to be mean!"[5] Walter
Sams strove to be one of these men.

Sams sought redemption of the South—and his own
fortune—by taking a path that took him away from his family
homeplace. "They tell the story about the time he had bought
the [Coca-Cola Bottling] territory in Muscogee, Oklahoma,"
remembers Jim Newland, husband of Sams's granddaughter
Dorothy. "He had told the family to move out there, but [on
the train to Oklahoma] he became friendly with a fellow who
was from somewhere in Mississippi. The man owned a
champion racehorse, and before he and the owner got off, Mr.
Sams had swapped the franchise for the horse," Newland
chuckles. So what did Sams do? "He intercepted the family
somewhere en route in Little Rock, Arkansas, and took 'em
back to Georgia." Back on his home state's soil, Walter Sams
bought into the Athens bottling operation.[6]

The Athens territory stretched over fifteen northeast
Georgia counties, anchored by Cornelia to the north and
Atlanta to the south. Leesburg and Lakeland, Florida,
franchises and a catering and vending subsidiary, Vend Inc.,
later expanded the reach of Sams's Coca-Cola bottling
interests. (The University of Georgia's Sanford Stadium

became an exclusive Sams outlet. Not only was it a high-volume, high-visibility venue, but product availability helped secure students from all over the state as loyal Coca-Cola drinkers.)[7]

Sams's net worth enjoyed a healthy boost, as did the estimation of his ability as a resourceful and able business-man. Having married Alla Dobbs, he acquired a powerful and influential kinsman in one Burney Dobbs, owner of a thriving coal and building materials concern and controller of the town's savings and loan institution. Dobbs maintained an ownership position in the soft drink company. Walter and Alla Sams had two sons, Albert and Walter Jr., both of whom were active contributors to the building of the franchise. Albert came into the family business in 1927, Walter Jr. in 1930. Albert was united in marriage to Miss Anita Burke; Walter Jr. married the daughter of University of Georgia professor Milton Jarnagin. The brothers were in turn joined in the business by their offspring, Albert Jr. ("Buddy") and Walter III ("Corky").[8]

Albert Sams took a lead in many preservation activities in Athens and was involved in the programs of the Rotary Club of Athens, serving as president of that civic organization. Walter Jr. was president of the Coca-Cola Bottlers of Georgia, and top officer of the local chamber of commerce and Community Chest as well as an elder at the First Presbyterian Church. Together, the brothers were effective in keeping the competition at bay, according to Jim Wimberly, regional manager of The Coca-Cola Company in Atlanta. One example of Albert's salesmanship: upon learning that a customer had replaced a Coke cooler with a competitive box at an outlet, Albert would drive up and approach the offending customer with an expression of abject mortification. "My old friend,"

Albert Sams would appeal, "what have I or any of my family ever done to make you do a terrible thing like this?" This kind of extremely "personal" service almost always brought reversal of the offending behavior and restoration of the product to its rightful place.[9]

From Agriculture to Industry

Born in 1880, Walter Sams witnessed and participated in the South's transition from an agrarian to an industrial society. In Sams's youth cotton mills sprang up in profusion along Georgia's "fall line," where abundant water—essential to the mills' operation—cascaded down from the mountains toward the coastal plain. The drive toward industrialization was on; every town wanted its own cotton mill. Even so, as historian C. Vann Woodward establishes in *Origins of the New South: 1877–1913*, the economy of postwar Georgia—and the South as a whole—essentially was a colonial one. Yankee overseers with textile industry experience were usually required to get the new cotton mills launched. But one of the first major textile plants in Georgia—Whitehall Mill—was begun in the late 1830s with exceptional homegrown leadership. At the helm of this enterprise was John White of Athens. The local financier, banker, and manufacturer built a Victorian Romanesque residence, White Hall, near the mill. It was deeded in 1936 to the University of Georgia, just as Sams's farm later would pass to the University.[10]

BY 1924, WALTER SAMS WAS LIVING AT 593 HILL STREET in a residential suburb known as Cobbham, in honor of the reigning family of Athens, the Cobbs. Patriarch Howell Cobb held a great many important positions: speaker of the U.S. House of Representatives, President Buchanan's secretary of the treasury, governor of Georgia, and major general in the Civil War. General T.R.R. Cobb had left his mark, as well, before falling in the Battle of Fredericksburg in 1863.[11] In the precincts of this historic presence, Sams was on his way as a civic and business leader.

The Coca-Cola plant first was located in 1906 at the corner of Hancock and Hull Streets in Athens's central business district, moving to a nearby site on Washington Street in 1916. By May 1928, according to the trade publication *Bottlers' Gazette*, Sams was president of the firm and had opened a new facility on Prince Avenue in an area fronting the Cobbham district (and diagonally across the street from the General T.R.R. Cobb House). With capacity production of 2,000 cases a day, the plant operated twelve trucks and employed thirty men. Historian Franklin M. Garrett wrote that occupancy actually was taken in 1927, and after five expansions an entire block was absorbed, including the historic Camak House.[12]

A strong supporting staff performed in the interests of the Sams enterprise. On a warm spring day in 1998 five of these cast members—with almost 200 years of combined experience—gathered to talk about the good old days. The host, Corky Sams, served up Coca-Cola in the eight-ounce package, the one most closely resembling the old six-and-one-half ounce container. The old timers remember what hard work went into running a bottling operation. Cecil "Deacon" Jones worked on the sales side of the business and recalls having only two annual holidays, Christmas Day and Thanksgiving, with no provisions for overtime pay. The consuming public stayed thirsty around the clock, it was reasoned, and Athens Coca-Cola had a mission of supplying the product at any special event, at virtually any time. Plant superintendent Frank Fowler, who took pride in seeing that product was available to deliver, was "on the floor" at all times.[13]

Jones tells of one Christmas day during the Depression when employees went in to claim their customary holiday bonus, allowing them to provide a decent Christmas to their families. This particular year had been a tough one. Times were bad, and Jones, among others, feared that Sams might not be able to come up with the money this time. Walter Sams called together his employees: "Well, you all know what a tough year it has been, but I'm happy to tell you I went to the bank and borrowed some money. Your bonus will be in the envelope on Millard's desk. Merry Christmas to all of you and yours!"[14]

Millard Epps was the man who checked in the drivers. On a hot summer's day some of them might not check in until 9 or 10 P.M. For drivers whose busy routes made them even later, it was convenient that Epps lived close by. Many a night drivers would proceed directly to Epps's house and then take him back to the plant for check-in. Deacon Jones jokes that some drivers were fond of gambling for small stakes during the day, often finding themselves without the bottler's money. But, thanks to a tolerant attitude by management, arrangements were made for the drivers to replace the funds at a later date.[15]

Budwine

While The Coca-Cola Bottling Company of Athens was wed to its premier product, in the early years Walter Sams also held local bottling rights for a product known as "Budwine." (It had at one time been known as "Bludwine," perhaps to suggest some kind of health-promoting properties.) Franchising rights for Budwine were held by the Costa family of Athens, local restaurant and soda fountain entrepreneurs. An alliance with the Costas was thought to be an advantageous one, and for a good many years "Budwine" was quite popular for the Sams family.

In the early part of the century soft drink brands were almost as numerous as the patent medicine remedies. As the end of the millennium approaches, however, most have disappeared from the scene as Coca-Cola and its principal rival—each with dozens of products sold under their auspices—have combined to control some eighty percent of the soft drink and refreshment market.[16]

STUDENTS AT THE UNIVERSITY WERE BIG CONSUMERS of Coca-Cola, but at times their playfulness could cause problems, recall Epps and Garland Kittle, former head of the bottler's sign shop. Upon those rare occasions when snow fell in Clarke County, the familiar red discs advertising Coke were targets for vandalism; it seems they were ideal for sledding down Baxter Hill from Alps Road. Problems arose, as well, when coolers would "jackpot." Nickels would come tumbling out of the machine to the delight of consumers, who predictably failed to turn over the windfall to the route salesman affected by the loss.[17]

Sometimes this playfulness was far less costly. Many customers can recall playing a game known as "faraway." At the base of each returnable glass bottle was a Coca-Cola point of origin, such as Bemidji, Minnesota; Montgomery, Alabama; or Baltimore, Maryland. As Coke drinkers would gather around the cooler, one would peer upward and call out: Laredo, Texas! Others would sing out their own bottling plant locations. The one whose bottle was from farthest off would win the modest pool of change wagered. It was such a modest transgression—and one so common to the community—that preachers never even seemed to condemn the practice in their Sunday hellfire-and-damnation sermons.[18]

SAID TO BE "CLOSE WITH HIS MONEY" AND FOCUSED on servicing the market in superior fashion, Walter Sams and his family were sometimes called paternalistic—but usually only by critics who failed to fathom their love for the business and for their employees. Workers were often given jobs that kept them around far beyond their productive years, some staying on until their eighties. They were members of the family in a very real sense. Frank Fowler was one such member, with a fifty-seven-year career as production manager with the plant. Fowler was also a self-taught inventor and innovator of the first order. By the time he retired, Fowler held fifty-three separate patents, most of these developed during his tenure with the company. Yet the Samses never claimed any ownership in the patents and encouraged

Fowler's inventiveness. Frank's son, Willie Fowler of Fowler Products, Inc., in Athens, comments, "In today's business environment you just wouldn't find that kind of helpful attitude on the part of ownership."[19] But, after all, the Coca-Cola plant benefitted vastly from Fowler's improvements. Fowler's skills as machinist, electrician, and welder saved the company thousands of dollars in replacement parts, time, and maintenance over the course of his long career.

Once Fowler recognized a need, he would plot possible solutions as he walked the short distance from his home on Prince Avenue to the plant. There he would sit down and invent equipment to do the job. His inventions included:

- Automatic bottle mixing machine
- Alarm for CO_2 gas pressure
- Bottle case printing machine
- Bottle washer
- Coin changer for vending machines
- Case rebanding machine
- Bottle code dater
- Automatic reclaimed crown reforming machine (during the material shortages of World War II)[20]

Some of Fowler's creations had application to businesses other than bottling. These included an automatic ice cream carton sealer, an automatic cracker sandwich making machine, and a "safti-vator" (a fire escape developed in the wake of Atlanta's 1946 Winecoff Hotel fire in which 119 guests perished), a fishing reel, an orange juice dispenser, and a rotary rheostat for wireless telegraphy.[21]

At some point in his career, the Samses and Fowler realized this talent for innovation deserved a range wider than was afforded by the plant or even the bottling industry as a whole. So it was with the family's encouragement that Hugh Fowler, another of Frank's sons, in 1952 formed a new company to facilitate the formation of Fowler Products. Frank Fowler retained his employment with the Sams family, with the understanding that he could bring his ideas and designs to the new firm with no interference.[22]

Operating in a low-key fashion, it's easy to overlook Fowler Products as an anachronism. The company is still headed by a Fowler — Frank's younger son, Willie (although for a few years in the 1980s the company was owned by a Baltimore concern), and the company still produces the same seemingly simple products and services — bottle fillers, juice cappers, remanufactured production machinery, and the like. But when you call the switchboard nowadays, you'll get a message in both English and Spanish; the company's success at devising better ways of meeting new needs has ensured its position as a corporation with global reach. The most striking applications of the Fowler know-how have been felt in the packaging field. Walk into the company's East Side headquarters and you'll see photographs of sealers and capping provided for products such as Mott's Apple Juice, Quaker Oats, and Kool-Aid, and for firms such as Baxter Laboratories, Merck, and Eastman Kodak.[23]

Walter Sams, who bought into the Coca-Cola business in 1922 using proceeds from the sale of a racehorse, typified the kind of entrepreneur and civic leader who contributed so much to the communities in his franchise territories. From farm to pharmacy to the Coca-Cola business — and back and forth several times — Sams built a respected and long-lived family of enterprises.

Endnotes

1 Ferrol Sams, *Run with the Horsemen* (Atlanta: Peachtree Publishers, 1982) 1-5.

2 Walter A. Sams III, interview by author, Athens, Georgia, 17 March 1998; biography of Walter A. Sams, The Coca-Cola Company Archives, Atlanta, Georgia.

3 Sams biography; Millard Epps, interview by author, Athens, Georgia, 8 April 1998; Sams interview.

4 Rick Dawson, interview by author, Athens, Georgia, 29 April 1998.

5 *Encyclopedia of Southern History* (Baton Rouge: Louisiana State University Press, 1979) 1102; Sams interview; Frances Taliaferro Thomas, *A Portrait of Historic Athens and Clarke County* (Athens: University of Georgia Press, 1992) 40, 170–171, 217, 219, 258; Mark Twain, as quoted by Mark Pendergrast in *For God, Country, and Coca-Cola* (New York: Scribner's, 1993) 15; C. Vann Woodward, *Tom Watson: Agrarian Rebel* (Savannah GA: Beehive Press, 1973) 100-101.

6 James L. Newland, interview by author, Athens, Georgia, 20 March 1998; Sams biography; Franklin M. Garrett, *The Coca-Cola Bottler*, April 1959, 123.

7 Albert B. Sams Jr., interview by author, Athens, Georgia, 11 November 1995.

8 Sams biography, The Coca-Cola Company Archives.

9 Warren Grice and E. Merton Coulter, *Georgia Through Two Centuries* (New York: Lewis Historical Publishing Company, 1965) 251–252; Albert B. Sams Jr., interview by author, Athens, Georgia, February 1995.

10 C. Vann Woodward, *Origins of the New South, 1877-1913* (Baton Rouge: Louisiana State University Press, 1971) 291-320; Louis de Vorsey Jr., "Early Water-Powered Industries in Athens and Clarke County," *Papers of the Athens Historical Society, Volume II* (Athens, 1979); and Frances Taliaferro Thomas, *A Portrait of Historic Athens and Clarke County* (Athens: University of Georgia Press, 1992).

11 John F. Stegeman, *These Men She Gave: A Civil War History of Athens, Georgia* (Athens: University of Georgia Press, 1964) 71–78.

12 *Bottlers' Gazette,* 15 May 1928, 163; Thomas, 51–56, 258. For a description of the plant and its architecture, see David Charles Cullison Jr., "J. W. Barnett: The Influence of the Architect and City Engineer on the Physical Development of Athens, Georgia," (master's thesis, University of Georgia, 1995). The Prince Avenue plant is now owned and operated by Coca-Cola Enterprises as a distribution center. And the Athens law firm of Winburn, Lewis, and Barrow now owns the Camak House, having restored it to its original glory. Traditionally among the leaders in advancing Athens's historic preservation, it was the Sams family that had sought listing of the Camak property on the National Register of Historic Places. Local government recognized such achievements by designating a major artery in the county Walter Sams Road. See Thomas, 258, and Patrick Neal, "Camak House: Victory for Preservation," *Athens Magazine,* April 1996, 72–81.

13 William C. Fowler, interview by author, Athens, Georgia, 2 April 1998; Walter A. Sams III, interview by author, Athens, Georgia, 8 April 1998; Frank Fowler Family Scrapbook, Athens, Georgia.

14 Cecil Jones, interview by author, Athens, Georgia, 9 April 1998.

15 Ibid.

16 Sams Biography, The Coca-Cola Company Archives; James Harvey Young, *The Toadstool Millionaires* (Princeton NJ: Princeton University Press, 1961); Robert D. Tollison, David P. Kaplan, and Richard S. Higgins, *Competition and Concentration* (Lexington MA: Lexington Books, 1991).

17 Garland Kittle, interview by author, Athens, Georgia, 8 April 1998.

18 Fowler interview.

19 Fowler Scrapbook.

20 Ibid.

21 Fowler interview.

22 Fowler Scrapbook.

23 Fowler interview.

7

THE HALEY FAMILY
OF ALBANY

The glass salesman would ride down old Highway 19 from Atlanta through Zebulon, Butler, Ellaville, Americus, Leesburg, and finally to Albany, the trade center of southwest Georgia. The crown salesman would make his way along the same two-lane highway. Both would be calling on brothers W. B. and J. T. Haley, hoping for one big order. Along the way, a pair of recurring sights stood out: Coca-Cola signs and pecan trees. Pecans and Coca-Cola.

In the Coca-Cola business "glass" meant bottles—and in those days the glass was in the form of the familiar Georgia green, six-and-one-half-ounce container with the hobble skirt design. "Crowns" were the metal, cork-lined caps on the bottles. For both the glass and the crown salesmen, a large order from the Haleys would keep them in the good graces of their sales managers for quite some time. After all, as it was often said, "The Haleys owned southwest Georgia." They owned it in terms of market share of the cold drinks consumed in the fields and on Main Street. And they physically owned the region, as well: the nation-leading pecan producers; one of the leading cattle farms; the dominant banking institutions;

the greatest proportion of farm acreage; and even the civic and cultural leadership positions.[1]

This powerful Coca-Cola territory in southwest Georgia was pioneered by William Banks Haley in 1903. His brother James, who already had set himself up with a franchise in Macon, persuaded W. B. to leave behind his grocery store clerking job in Chattanooga and go south to bottle Coke. For the next several decades, W. B. Haley served the public interest of his territory. He was mayor of Albany for sixteen years, or "about anytime he wanted to accept the job," according to his retired sales manager Buford Collins.[2] He was president of the chamber of commerce four times, served on the city and county school boards, and was president and a charter member of The Rotary Club of Albany.[3] Upon his death in 1950, the editor emeritus of *The Albany Herald* (of which W. B.'s son Herbert Haley was part owner) wrote the following in an editorial captioned "Banks Haley: A Great Builder":

> Few men have meant as much to Albany as he meant. Few have had more widely diversified interests, and none has shown a more abiding faith in this section. From the time he came to Albany, 'Banks' Haley was a successful business man, and his vision led him into many enterprises, but his community and the section surrounding it always had first call on his capital and his urge to build....[H]is community loyalty was strongly reflected in his unfailing loyalty to his friends, who were to be found among all classes.[4]

SALES MANAGER BUFORD COLLINS, A FORTY-EIGHT-year veteran of the Albany bottler, worked for both W. B. and for Herbert (who took over in 1950), so he is well versed in the bottlers' marketing philosophies — which included the retention of the nickel Coke. "We did hold that price line for a long time," Collins says of the savvy business tactic.[5]

The Haley Group of plants was one of the very last to break the rock-bottom wholesale price per case that kept the retail level at five cents. Competitors howled, but the tactic amounted to a major weapon in the Haley arsenal. Competitors found themselves stuck at a wholesale plateau with significantly smaller shares of the market, and thus bereft of resources for adequate advertising or plant improvements.[6] Lacking the Haley's volume and market shares, the competitors scarcely could mount a challenge.

Of course, there was a time when a mere nickel was virtually the universal retail price for the drink. At that rate everyone could afford refreshment, even in the poverty-racked days of the Great Depression. Jim Wimberly, a former corporate vice president for The Coca-Cola Company, elaborates: "No matter how broke a man was, no matter if he was out of work, he could just about always scrape up five cents and ask a fellow, 'Let me buy you a Coke.'"[7]

The bottle of Coca-Cola had been in the public eye for two or three decades, increasingly visible through advertising and vast distribution. For the Atlanta-based parent company, gallon sales to the bottlers were increasing incrementally. Relative to the economy as a whole, the Coca-Cola System (as it has been called by Coca-Cola Company leaders in recent times) was in great shape, aided by the fact that the bottling business was a cash business. Consumers pushed nickels into vending machines or went to "fillin' stations" and reached in a cooler for the drink, submerged in icy water. Route salesmen poured the nickels into the heavy leather bags that were a part of their equipment. The salesmen charged eighty cents for a case of twenty-four; at five cents a bottle, the retailer was bringing in $1.20 a case—a fifty percent margin, far better than the mark-up on most retail items. And so it was that at the end of a long day of making Coke available to hot, thirsty Georgians, the route men descended on the bottling plant to check in with the cash and obtain verification of the amount of product sold. It was a rare day when the owner or the sales manager was not on hand for the checking-in ritual. As one owner explained, "You trust your people, but you don't want to put temptation in their way; can't have 'em stealing from you."[8]

With foreclosures and bankruptcies at high tide during the Depression, businesses and banks were being ruined right and left. But the "friendly neighbor who bottles Coca-Cola" was in a prime position; his was the most reliable cash-generating business in virtually any Georgia town. If early bottlers had shown gumption by acquiring a franchise—especially during the initial decade (1900-1910)—the prudent ones, such as the Haleys, demonstrated even more gumption by making shrewd investments in sundry non-bottling ventures. John Holman, Herbert Haley's vice president over bottling operations until the 1985 sale of the business,[9] ticked off a lengthy roster of Haley investments throughout the region, including:

- •Haley Farms, with its 40,000 acres of farmland and once the world's-largest improved pecan farm
- •Banks in Cuthbert, Cordele, Albany, Bainbridge, Blakely, Fort Gaines, and Dawson

- Ford automobile dealerships
- Oil distribution companies, including those handling Shell Oil products
- Albany's leading hotel, The Gordon
- *The Albany Herald* newspaper, a dominant daily read throughout the region
- Ten Coca-Cola plants, owned in varying degree by either the W. B. Haley or J. T. Haley families and located in Albany, Cuthbert, Moultrie, Leesburg, Richland, Americus, Pelham, Americus, Cordele, and Fitzgerald

Despite the Haleys's wealth of investments, John Holman adds that "they all were so modest; too, acted like they didn't have a dime. People appreciated that about them."[10]

While W. B. and his son Herbert were deeply immersed in the bottling business (as were sons Joel, who ran the Cordele plant, and James, who ran Moultrie), J. T. Haley and his son, J. T. Jr., were recognized more widely for their leadership in banking circles. With W. B.'s death in 1950, J. T. Jr.'s in 1955, and J. T. Sr.'s in 1956, by mid-century Herbert Haley had inherited control over a large and complicated enterprise.[11] "If J. T. Jr. had lived," concedes John Holman, "a lot of things might have been different."[12]

Herbert Haley's was a background not commonly found among those running Coca-Cola bottling operations in those days. A graduate of Georgia Tech, Herbert held two advanced degrees—a master's and a doctorate, both in mechanical engineering—from the Massachusetts Institute of Technology. His great strengths were in the technical side of the business, perhaps explaining the thorough nature with which he made decisions. As Holman quotes Herbert as saying, "When a problem confronts me, I try to think of every possible solution and its implications not only for the business, but for our employees."

Herbert Haley went against the grain in several other of his policies, as well. When Coke bottlers finally made an effort to stem the tide of Pepsi-Cola's ten and twelve ounce volume advantage—as opposed to Coke's "regular size" six-and-one-half ounce package—Herbert opted for a squattier, less elongated package than most of his fellow Coke bottlers; Herbert knew that the taller bottle would tip over on the bottling line. When The Coca-Cola Company began to push a twenty-six ounce drink, most Coke bottlers stayed away from introducing it in droves. Not Herbert Haley. He knew his consumers' profiles; farm hands and industrial workers had a preference for the twenty-six ounce, a drink that would last them through the second sandwich in their lunch box. In fact, there was only one advertisement on page one of *The Albany Herald* each day, and that one was for the twenty-six ouncer.[13]

While the centerpiece of the Haley empire was the bottling business, the Haleys did not neglect their civic responsibilities. Herbert Haley was chairman of the Dougherty County school board and was a trustee of Wesleyan College, the women's institution up the road in Macon. J. T. was on the board of the Central of Georgia Railway Company and president of the Georgia Bankers Association. A sketch of J. T. in *Georgia Through Two Centuries* states that he was "a driving force, and stabilizing influence, in every progressive movement that affected this section, working for maintenance of farm incomes and obtaining the use of pecans in the Federal school lunch program." W. B. managed to free the city of Albany from debt while serving as mayor. *The Story of Georgia* calls W. B. one of "the most prominent, influential and successful figures in the social, civic, and business affairs" of his region, approvingly citing his leading role in the realm of public service. Both J. T. and W. B. were on the board of Fulton National Bank in Atlanta, where their Coca-Cola Company friends and allies, Harrison Jones and Pope F. Brock, were chairmen of the board.[14]

So, if "the Haleys owned southwest Georgia," future generations in this part of the state were beneficiaries of a great many Haley dividends of progress and prosperity.

Endnotes

---

[1] Franklin M. Garrett, Haley Biographical Sketch, The Coca-Cola Company Archives, Atlanta, Georgia.

[2] Buford Collins, interview by author, Albany, Georgia, 28 January 1998. Collins himself was vice-mayor for twenty-three years, most of it during the bottling presidency of Herbert Haley, W. B.'s son.

[3] Walter G. Cooper, *The Story of Georgia* (New York: American Historical Society, 1937) 278.

[4] H. T. McIntosh, obituary of W. B. Haley, *Albany Herald*, 17 January 1950, reprinted in "W. B. Haley, Pioneer Bottler, Succumbs to Heart Attack," *Coca-Cola Bottler*, September 1950, 28.

[5] Collins interview. Adds Collins, "Whenever I complain that this or that sure is expensive, my wife will say, 'Oh, Collins, you're still living in the time of the nickel Coca-Cola.'"

[6] Harrison Jones II, interview by author, Atlanta, Georgia, December 1997; John Holman, interview by author, Albany, Georgia, 28 January 1998. Collins interview.

[7] James W. Wimberly, interview by author, Atlanta, Georgia, February 1996.

[8] Anonymous Coca-Cola bottler, conversation with author, Southwest Bottler Sales Development Region, ca. 1963.

[9] The Albany plant was sold to Coca-Cola Consolidated, headquartered in Charlotte, North Carolina, in 1985.

[10] Holman interview.

[11] Ibid. See also Warren Grice, *Georgia Through Two Centuries* (New York: Lewis Historical Publishing Company, 1966) 287–288.

[12] Holman interview. In addition to the internal changes brought about by the passing of three of the franchise's key players, the 1960s were a turbulent decade for Albany and Southwest Georgia as a whole. The Albany Movement and Dr. Martin Luther King Jr. moved to center stage in the community to challenge long-standing segregation policies.

[13] Holman interview; Wimberly interview.

[14] Grice, *Georgia Through Two Centuries*, 287–288.

Benjamin F. Thomas and Joseph B. Whitehead of Chattanooga, Tennessee, were granted the first bottling rights—at no charge—from the Coca-Cola Company's Asa Candler in 1899.

Joseph B. Whitehead (*The Coca-Cola Company Archives*)

Asa Candler (*Atlanta History Center*)

Benjamin F. Thomas
(*The Benwood Foundation*)

John T. Lupton joined
forces with Benjamin
Thomas and Joseph
Whitehead to operate
Coca-Cola's bottling
operations. In 1900, Lupton
and Whitehead launched
what would become the
Atlanta Coca-Cola Bottling
Company at the corner of
Edgewood Avenue and
Courtland Street.
(*The Coca-Cola Company
Archives*)

The Chattanooga Coca-Cola Bottling Plant, ca. 1950. The large billboard atop the plant clearly expresses the wishes of the plant's operators. (*The Coca-Cola Company Archives*)

George Thomas Hunter, nephew of and successor to Benjamin F. Thomas and his Chattanooga bottling operation. Perhaps Hunter's greatest legacy is Chattanooga's Benwood Foundation. Benwood and the Lyndhurst Foundation (created to honor the memory of fellow bottler John T. Lupton) together claim more than $232 million in assets and are largely responsible for the revitalization of Chattanooga. (*The Coca-Cola Company Archives*)

Arthur L. Montgomery (below), the last man in his family to head up the Atlanta Coca-Cola Bottling Company (above) and one of "the big three," along with Mayor Ivan Allen Jr. and Mills B. Lane, who brought major-league sports to Atlanta. (*Atlanta History Center*)

Brothers Willie (left) and Alfred Lee Barron (below), community leaders in their hometown of Rome, Georgia, and throughout their bottling territory in Northwest Georgia. Their father, F. S. Barron, obtained bottling rights for the region in 1901. Their city's first and a more modern Rome-area bottling plants are shown (next page).
Photographs: The Coca-Cola Company Archives

First Rome bottling
plant (*Collection of
Frank W. Barron*)

Rome-area bottling plant (*Collection of Frank W. Barron*)

Columbus Roberts Sr., the Coca-Cola bottler for Columbus, Georgia, donated more than $2.5 million in his lifetime—$55 million in today's dollars. Macon's Mercer University was one of his primary beneficiaries. (*The Coca-Cola Company Archives*)

Walter A. Sams purchased the Athens, Georgia, bottling franchise after trading an Oklahoma franchise for a racehorse. A farmer at heart, Sams was known to close the plant and take employees out to his farm to bale hay. (*Collection of Albert Sams Jr., Athens, Georgia*)

W. Banks Haley, president of the Albany (Ga.) Coca-Cola Bottling Company, was quite the civic leader in the Southwest Georgia city, serving as mayor for sixteen years, as well as a member of the chamber of commerce and city and county school boards. (*The Coca-Cola Company Archives*)

George Cobb Sr. (right) ran the West Georgia bottling territory that included the towns of West Point and LaGrange. (*The Coca-Cola Company Archives*)

Interior of the LaGrange plant in 1908, its first year of operation. (*The Coca-Cola Company Archives*)

George Cobb Jr. succeeded his father in 1930 in the West Georgia bottling territory. (*The Coca-Cola Company Archives*)

Edward Delony Sledge, the director of advertising for The Coca-Cola Company from the 1940s through the 1960s, worked to convince the bottlers that their hard-earned dollars were being well spent. Sledge is the gentleman seated among his mustachioed staff above, and below.
(*The Coca-Cola Company Archives*)

W. C. Bradley of Columbus, Georgia—onetime chair of The Coca-Cola Company and mentor to future Coke Chairman Robert W. Woodruff. His family's Bradley-Turner Foundation is to Columbus what the Woodruff Foundation is to Atlanta. (*The Atlanta History Center*)

Harrison Jones, chairman of The Coca-Cola Company from 1942 to 1952. Said Atlanta bottler Arthur Montgomery of Jones, "He could make you laugh; he could make you cry; and he darn sure could inspire you to sell Coca-Cola!" (*Collection of Harrison Jones II, Atlanta, Georgia*)

C. Veazey Rainwater boasted the longest continuing service record in the history of Coca-Cola bottling—seventy-one years. Rainwater was a key player in Coca-Cola's Standardization Committee, which helped create consistency in the company's distinctive bottling plant architecture, as seen in these photos of the Tifton and LaGrange operations. (*The Coca-Cola Company Archives*)

Tifton Plant   LaGrange Plant

The first and second conventions of the Coca-Cola bottlers, 1909 and 1910. Sponsored by The Coca-Cola Company, it was the company's hope that the bottlers would return from the conventions refreshed and full of zeal for selling the beverage. The Coca-Cola Bottlers Association was formed in 1914. (*The Coca-Cola Company Archives*)

From the early days of mule-drawn wagons to standardized delivery trucks, the bottlers have worked to keep Coca-Cola, as the advertising tag line touted, "within an arm's length of desire." (*The Coca-Cola Company Archives*)

Since the first outdoor advertising message in 1894 — a painted wall
outside of a Cartersville, Georgia, pharmacy — advertising has been a
key component to The Coca-Cola Company's and the bottlers' success.
(*Dean Cox, Young Brothers Pharamacy, Cartersville, Georgia*)

These woodcuts depict a typical Coca-Cola bottling plant, early and mid-twentieth century. (*The Benwood Foundation*)

Coca-Cola advertising, such as this print ad from 1940, often emphasized the convenience of drinking bottled Coca-Cola at home. (*The Coca-Cola Company Archives*)

Ads touting bottled Coca-Cola, 1950s. (*The Coca-Cola Company Archives*)

The Coca-Cola bottle itself was designed to be as distinctive as the drink inside, as this 1916 print ad attests. The bottlers' initials were often blown into the glass as a sign of pride.
Ad: *The Coca-Cola Company Archives*

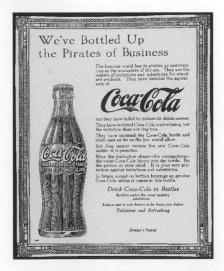

We've Bottled Up the Pirates of Business

The business world has its pirates, as unscrupulous as the marauders of the sea. They are the makers of imitations and substitutes for standard products. They have imitated the appearance of

Coca-Cola

but they have failed to imitate its deliciousness

They have imitated Coca-Cola's advertising, but the imitation does not ring true.

They have imitated the Coca-Cola bottle and label—just as far as the law would allow.

But they cannot imitate the new Coca-Cola bottle—it is patented.

Note the distinctive shape—the corrugations—the name Coca-Cola blown into the bottle. Fix the picture in your mind. It is your sure protection against imitations and substitutes.

In future, accept no bottled beverage as genuine Coca-Cola unless it comes in this bottle.

Drink Coca-Cola in Bottles
Bottled under the most sanitary conditions

Keep a case in your home—order from your dealer
Delicious and Refreshing

(Dealer's Name)

Coca-Cola bottling plants at work (and facing page). The challenge for The Coca-Cola Company, according to chairman Robert W. Woodruff: "What can you and I do to make Coca-Cola available to anyone, anywhere in the world, whenever they want one, and be certain that it tastes just like the last Coca-Cola they drank?" (*Atlanta History Center*)

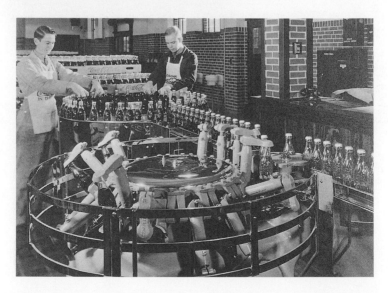

The influence of Robert W. Woodruff, longtime Coca-Cola Company Chairman, extended far beyond the walls of his company. His Robert W. Woodruff Foundation has contributed mightily to healthcare, education, and the arts throughout the Southeast, and has acted as a role model for other foundations rooted in "Coca-Cola money." (*Atlanta History Center*)

A 1928 Coca-Cola cooler. In 1910–1912 George Cobb of the LaGrange-West Point bottling operation secured a patent on the first coin-operated dispensing machine, spawning an entire generation of sophisticated coolers, such as this one, and spurring the growth of the "cold-bottle market." (*The Coca-Cola Company Archives*)

Harold Hirsch, longtime
legal counsel to The Coca-
Cola Company, often
represented the bottlers, as
well. A former University
of Georgia football player,
he helped forge the strong
link between collegiate
athletics and Coca-Cola.
(*The Coca-Cola Company
Archives*)

8

THE COBB FAMILY OF LAGRANGE AND WEST POINT

Among relations in the same business, disputes and alienation arise from time to time. But George S. Cobb Sr. and brother-in-law Columbus Roberts rose above such disagreement. Their business? Coca-Cola bottling, of course. In 1908 Cobb bought from the Columbus, Georgia-based Roberts the bottling territory in west Georgia comprising LaGrange and West Point, as well as the Valley area across the Chattahoochee River into Alabama.[1]

Cobb had grown up in nearby Opelika, Alabama, the son of dentist John Cobb, who died when George was just sixteen. Forced to work, George Cobb landed jobs as a telegraph messenger, for a trucking concern, for a cotton broker, and, just briefly, for Roberts's LaGrange bottling plant. Little did Cobb know then that one day the plant would be his and a worldwide leader in per capita consumption.[2]

In 1910-1912, George Cobb secured a patent on the first coin-operated dispensing machine, the "Vend-All Nickel in Slot Vending Machine." This twelve-bottle model (which Cobb posted in front of his plant) spawned an entire generation of increasingly sophisticated coolers and foreshadowed the dominance George S. Cobb and his son George Jr. would achieve in what became known in the industry as the cold bottle market.[3]

About the same time, Cobb recorded possibly another first for the young bottling business—he purchased a ten horse-power Reo Truck for deliveries. In 1915, a second Reo was added to the burgeoning Cobb "fleet." Up until this point territories had been served exclusively by mule- or horse-drawn wagons. In fact, most franchises were designed to be about fifty miles across so that they could be traversed in a day by a wagon and driver. But, despite the promise and potential of this new mode of transportation, the mules kept their jobs. On the crude, muddy roads of the time, the animals were needed for pulling the Reos out of quagmires all over the territory.[4]

Despite the mud, Cobb's revolutionary new distribution method would eventually be seen as a breakthrough. "Trucks came, and with them a better class of salesmen," Cobb stated. "But it was a long time before paved and better roads, which were necessary, could be fully utilized." In like turn, since the early 1950s, the interstate highway system has brought about vast economies of scale in distribution. It is as easy now for Coca-Cola to be dropped off in an Atlanta-to-Charlotte run as it was for George Cobb to transport product across the river to the Valley in Alabama.

Bottling line volume has improved apace, too. In the early years of the century Cobb's foot-powered bottling machines had a capacity, he wrote, of "two dozen cases per day of ten hours." Often complaining of a "lack of good help," Cobb wrote "of the many hired there were but few that could or would master the operations of the Foot Power. We were at the mercy of these [workers],…so when they decided to take off and go to a ball game, why…you couldn't do anything about it." Cobb was a hard worker, and he was frustrated by those who didn't share his work ethic.[5]

It wasn't just machinery and a dedicated work force that Cobb concentrated upon; promotion and marketing played a large role in his success, as well. When he felt newspaper advertising was not delivering enough customers, the industry pioneer went visual. "I made slides, and these were thrown on the screens of moving picture theaters," recalls Cobb. Saving Coke bottle caps was another way for consumers to become involved. "Save Crowns; They Get Premiums" was a popular Cobb slogan; premiums included clocks, knives, purses, pencils, and matches.[6]

ON THE INAUGURAL TRIP OF THE AB&A RAILROAD from Brunswick to Atlanta, Coca-Cola Company founder Asa G. Candler was among the dignitaries aboard. Earlier, Candler had written Cobb asking that he arrange to serve ice cold Coca-Cola to the notables at LaGrange. When the train went through Manchester, west of the city, Cobb and his crew brought lots of Coke aboard and iced it down. By the time the entourage arrived in LaGrange, the Coca-Cola was ice cold and ready to serve—along with Cobb's advertising novelties. Obviously pleased with the Manchester-to-LaGrange locomotive run, Cobb asked Candler "what he thought of our job of serving" and merchandising. The Great Man replied, "Cobb, it looked like a Coca-Cola Special!" The pioneer bottler had demonstrated he could sell, merchandise, and promote with the best of them.[7]

Another stratagem—an oil cloth streamer proclaiming ICE COLD COCA-COLA FOR SALE HERE—paid off handsomely, as well. Cobb urged storekeepers to put the product in tubs of ice and hang the streamer. Soon, customers were becoming irate if they encountered Coke at less than the recommended forty degrees. By the early 1980s the response was more than evident—a per-capita consumption rate of nearly 700 each year, or nearly two bottles daily for each man, woman, and child in the territory.[8]

In at least one promotion urging consumers to "save valuable crowns" and redeem them for prizes, however, Cobb's innovative strategy backfired. As the plant redeemed prizes on the basis of weight, young boys were discovered loading down their containers of bottle caps with rocks and other heavy objects. In a related development, after the company disposed of the redeemed crowns in the river, local boys retrieved them and re-redeemed them for a "double-dip" of prizes. But it was not until 1965 that Coca-Cola bottlers, including Cobb, staged the most successful under-the-crown promotion ever. The likenesses of National Football League players were placed on the underside, and thousands of fans packed bottling plants across the nation to enter into the competition where they matched the players on a game card. (Presumably these latter-day bottlers knew better than to dispose of the crowns by dumping them into lakes, streams, and other bodies of water.)[9]

GEORGE COBB SPOKE OF MANY CHANGES DURING HIS forty-seven years in the bottling industry. His reminiscences were published in 1976 for a special bicentennial edition of *The Valley Times-News*; an excerpt follows:

I got started in what is now called the gay '90s. I missed the gay part. There was quite a shortage of cash money in those days and especially among the families of professional men. My father was a dentist. His town patients did not seem to pay him but little at all, and patients on the farms paid him mostly in what they produced...a lot of sweet potatoes and kindling wood, etc.

In May 1905 I accepted a position with my brother-in-law, Columbus Roberts, at Columbus, Georgia. My salary to start was $1,200 per year, with the privilege of buying an interest in the Columbus Company. I did not have any great visions of Coca-Cola's future at that time. I had saved a little money and did buy a small interest. In 1908, we incorporated the LaGrange and West Point territories. I moved to LaGrange. Prior to this time both the territories had been leased on a royalty basis....They were granted what was known as a subfranchise. The royalty was 30 cents per gallon. Coca-Cola (syrup) at that time was $1.20 to first line bottlers, and the lessees paid $1.50. In a few years I became sole owner of this territory and secured a direct franchise from the parent, Coca-Cola Bottling Company of Atlanta....In 1909 I moved to West Point, which became my permanent home.

Soon after these first five or so years in the business, Cobb was sold on its potential. Today so many people think that Coca-Cola was a gold mine, even to begin with, but that is far from the truth. It has been a continuous fight from Mr. Asa Candler's early days until the present time. I know of no business that has been built up in similar manner and with so much concerted work and effort....All would get together in friendly contact and study, hoping to gain... knowledge or [a] scheme...that would make progress in the Coca-Cola business. A Coca-Cola Bottler with all of his family and loyal employees is one of the strongest business influences in any community, and what a tremendous asset to the Parent Company! The early days were hard, very hard, but I enjoyed it.[10]

His neighbors soon would learn more about the franchise-holder's tenacity and competitiveness. One local firm bottled an imitation of Coca-Cola and sold it as the real thing. The renegade bottler eventually was stopped, but in the meantime George S. Cobb decided to have his initials, "G.S.C.," blown directly into the bottles. Consumers would tell vendors, "Nah, let me have one of those G.S.C. Coca-Cola's!" Some think the inspiration for this tactic was Asa G. Candler, who ran the legend, "Bottled under authority of Asa G. Candler" on the bottlers' containers. Either way, it worked.[11]

As the business matured, other bottlers began to look to the Cobbs for more innovation and industry leadership. The Cobb operations pioneered the sampling of new product, even during the Depression and World War II gas rationing. The plants concentrated on public schools where they would have the product available—either through coolers or at school cafeterias—at a clip of ninety percent or greater coverage. George S. Cobb Sr. was a leader, as well, in sampling by way of six-bottle cartons. In 1953, when a new plant was dedicated in West Point, close to forty percent of the city's population showed up to celebrate—and drink Coke. As the area became a textile center, plant personnel made certain Coca-Cola was available. In a time when a grocery store or a gas station might be serviced by Coca-Cola bottlers once or twice a week, the cotton mills got daily re-stockings of product.[12]

George Cobb Jr. remembers that in 1930 when he became general manager, succeeding his father, the mills were especially hard hit; those still open typically were working a one-and-one-half day week. "There were thirty-three straight months of losses," recalled the younger Cobb. It was a stern test for the young Emory graduate, one who had developed a fondness for and a grasp of advertising and sales as business manager/advertising manager of *The Emory Wheel*, the campus newspaper. But after some hard work and applied salesmanship, the "Depression proof" refreshment with the five-cent purchase price grew in popularity. And the textile industry — and their workers thirst — survived and came back stronger than ever.

Schools, industrial plants, recreational areas: all were cultivated. Loyal Coke drinkers were won over in their formative years in the schools, growing into adults who enjoyed the refreshment at home, at work, and at play. Howard H. "Bo" Callaway, a leader in public life on both the state and national levels, remembers well growing up in LaGrange. Along with the rest of his fourth-grade class, Bo marched behind their teacher — a Miss Hazlett — to the Coke plant. The Cobbs and their loyal employees exposed the children to the hygienic perfection of the rapid-speed bottling line and ushered the teacher and her charges into a meeting room to see a movie about the business. Then came the presentation of a trademarked Coca-Cola red pencil, a tablet, and a golden rule ruler...all followed by an ice-cold Coca-Cola for everyone! Callaway says the event is one of his most cherished memories. And, as it turned out, almost every bottler in the country began to provide such plant visits for their own fourth graders.[13]

Bo Callaway points, as well, to the community leadership roles assumed by bottlers across America. Like the Cobbs, he says, "almost everywhere they were presidents of the Rotary Club, underwrote Little League baseball, were stalwarts of the chambers of commerce, and tireless advocates for economic and industrial development." Father and son were indeed presidents of the Rotary Club, as well as stewards in the Methodist church and prominent in the affairs of Methodist-related LaGrange College. George Jr. was consecutively chairman of the institution's executive committee and board of trustees.[14]

In 1944 the family founded the Cobb Foundation "to plow back into our territory some of the profits that our customers made possible by purchasing our product." One act of generosity was to underwrite what became the Cobb Memorial Archives at the H. Grady Bradshaw Chambers County Library, in memory of George Sydney and Edna Levy Cobb. "With Daddy, what mattered most were the church, the college, and the library," says Lillian Cobb Cauble of West Point, daughter of George Jr. and Lillian Edmondson Cobb. Cauble underlines that the foundation's fundamental mission is to serve the needs of the area and those who were—or are—the people of the Cobb family's old franchise territory.[15]

THE VEND-ALL PATENT WAS YET ANOTHER MARKET-ing innovation for the Cobbs, one that would eventually changes the direction of the family's business. The Vend-All dispenser—or cooler, in industry parlance—opened up possibilities in vending in general, eventually leading to a full-line vending operation: serving up Coke, of course, but also coffee, sandwiches, hot soups, snacks, crackers, candy, pastries, and even competitive beverages. But George Cobb Jr. felt slighted over how "the coffee break" had become an American institution—and how the custom should have been known as "a Coke break." Cobb would pre-empt the competition and sell the roasted and brewed product alongside Coke for refreshment.[16]

Lillian Cobb Cauble and her husband, D. Z., moved from bottling operations to emphasize the vending operation in the scheme of things. Their son, Zim, now runs Vend-All. Lillian's sister, Sydney Cobb Smith, lives in Marietta with her husband, William D. Smith, and both served on the respective boards of the bottling entities.[17]

In 1930, George Cobb Sr. turned the reins over to his only son, George Jr., after leading the enterprise for thirty-one years. (George Cobb Sr. died in 1952.) George Jr. took hold and guided the firm's fortunes for forty-seven years before becoming board chairman in 1977. Sid Foster took over the plant in 1977 and ran it until it was sold in 1989 to Coca-Cola United.[18]

Coca-Cola United assumed ownership of a prime territory in LaGrange and West Point, one whose father-and-son team of leaders could boast of many achievements and many firsts in the industry. The mechanical marvel, George Cobb Sr., carved out that area and laid the groundwork for the sales-oriented George Jr. to saturate the market.

On 13 October 1982, the Newcomen Society in North America gathered at a private Atlanta club to honor the Cobb family for their faithful stewardship and enlightened corporate citizenship. LaGrange College president Waights G. Henry Jr. delivered the principal address that evening, pointing to the many achievements of the Cobb family as well as their faith in the community and their exemplary character. In doing so, he took special notice of how the plants' ownership moved in proactive fashion to provide a comprehensive retirement plan for employees — three years before Social Security was signed into law.[19]

The success of this Coca-Cola franchise, it might be said, always was several paces ahead of even the most enlightened players in the world of commerce and industry. As Robert W. Woodruff and H. B. Nicholson often claimed, the Coca-Cola business has been a part of "a passing parade." And if that be the case, as many will argue, the Cobb family of LaGrange and West Point marched at the head of the column and carried the standard proudly. Their neighbors and customers in the territory cheered as they passed in review.[20]

Endnotes

1 *Lanett* (Ala.) and *West Point* (Ga.) *Valley-Times News*, 3 June 1976, D1.

2 George Cobb biography, The Coca-Cola Company Archives, Atlanta, Georgia.

3 *Valley-Times News*.

4 Ibid. In those days, the wagon drivers were not accorded the same salesman status as the truck drivers later would. Among other things, according to Cobb, these men "had to look after and care for their mules and wagons, and some of these early drivers were a sorry lot."

5 *Valley-Times News*.

6 Ibid.

7 Ibid.

8 Waights G. Henry Jr., "Tributary to a Golden Stream," address to Newcomen Society in North America, Atlanta, Georgia, 13 October 1982.

9 *Valley-Times News*.

10 Ibid.

11 Ibid.; Pat Watters, *Coca-Cola: An Illustrated History* (Garden City NY: Doubleday, 1977) 63.

12 *The Coca-Cola Bottler*, 5 October 1977, 6; *Bottler*, January 1956, 7; Cobb biography; and Kenneth Coleman and Charles Stephen Gurr, *Dictionary of Georgia Biography* (Athens: University of Georgia Press, 1982) 149–153.

13 Howard H. Callaway, interview by author, LaGrange, Georgia, 11 February 1998.

14 Callaway interview; Henry, "Tributary."

15 Lillian Cobb Cauble, interview by author, West Point, Georgia, 8 March 1998.

16 Cauble interview.

17 The Coca-Cola Company Archives.

[18] *Bottler*, January 1956; Bill Hensel, Public and Media Relations, The Coca-Cola Company, interview by author, Atlanta, Georgia, 1 April 1998.

Coca-Cola United is one of three significant megabottlers, along with Coca-Cola Enterprises and Coca-Cola Consolidated. The Coca-Cola Company maintains a substantial ownership position—about forty-four percent—in one of the trio, Coca-Cola Enterprises, which does almost sixty-seven percent of the business in the United States.

[19] Henry, "Tributary."

[20] Harmon B. Nicholson, address to Newcomen Society in North America, New York, 18 December 1953.

9

E. DELONY SLEDGE:
BOOSTING THE BOTTLERS' SALES
THROUGH ADVERTISING

Two days before Christmas 1996, Coca-Cola Company
Chairman Roberto C. Goizueta gathered several of his company's retired officers for an intimate luncheon. The setting
was Goizueta's executive dining room atop Coca-Cola's
Atlanta headquarters. Among the chief guests was a veteran
of the business, James W. Wimberly, who oversaw bottler
sales in the Southeast. His eyesight no longer permitted him
to pore over gallonage sales records and cooperative marketing agreements with bottlers, as once was his practice. But
Jim Wimberly—University of Georgia, class of 1940, native of
Waynesboro, Georgia—listened intently, anticipating the
announcement of some historic breakthrough for the business.

Goizueta began: "A billion hours ago human life appeared
on earth. A billion minutes ago the Beatles performed on The
Ed Sullivan Show." The Cuban-born chairman of Georgia's
largest and most globally recognized commercial entity
paused, and then continued. "A billion Coca-Colas ago was
yesterday morning."[1]

PERHAPS IT WAS FREDERICK ALLEN'S BOOK TITLE
that best characterized the accomplishments of the pioneers in
the soft drink business — *Secret Formula: How Brilliant
Marketing and Relentless Salesmanship Made Coca-Cola the Best
Known Product in the World*. And without question one of the
best-remembered, yet rarely profiled, pioneers in the industry
was Edward Delony Sledge, a native of Athens, Georgia.[2]

The Athenian was an intellectual steeped in the lore and
languages of the classics and the history and traditions of the
American South. Sledge was the grandson of Confederate
Major General Howell Cobb, who left President Buchanan's
cabinet to preside over the organizing assembly of a new
nation and then led "Cobb's Legion" against the enemy.
Virtually every position of trust within the gift of the people of
Georgia was his: superior court judge, state representative,
member and speaker of the U.S. House of Representatives,
U.S. senator, and governor of the state. Being born into the
Cobb family provided quite a legacy for Delony Sledge. But
while his credentials were impeccable, it was his intellect and
ability that marked him as one destined for great things in
life.[3]

Sledge loved his hometown with its classic columns and
university campus. After a year at the University of Georgia,
where he became a member of the Sigma Alpha Epsilon social
fraternity, young Delony Sledge entered World War I and
attained the rank of captain while assigned to an artillery unit.
But like many a Georgian from the state's smaller cities and
towns, it was in the capital city of Atlanta that Delony Sledge
made his own mark.[4]

He attended Georgia Tech and received a degree in civil
engineering. Associates relate that Sledge was at times a forest
ranger, a western cowboy, and an Atlanta real estate man. In

1933, while selling for a local sign company, he called on The Coca-Cola Company; they hired him away to work in their advertising department. Sledge became ad director and vice-president before retiring at age sixty-five.[5]

During his thirty-two years with Coca-Cola, Sledge's marketing efforts took on a highly professional look, and his budget became one of the largest in the world of advertising. In many ways, say those who knew Sledge professionally, it was "the century of Sledge." In a 1963 profile, *Advertising Age* called Sledge "one of the great advertising managers of the past fifty years." The influential trade organ added that he "carries in his head all anyone needs to know about the soft drink and advertising business — and the marriage, and the children produced by the two."[6]

E. Delony Sledge's tremendous influence upon the beverage's advertising and marketing thrust — coupled with the relentless salesmanship of the bottler body — provided much of the impetus for industry leadership. At least it did in the minds of Coca-Cola bottlers everywhere, especially those in Georgia. In a business known for its competitive warfare at the point of sale, it was the howitzers of massive media advertising that took a modest concoction of sugar, carbonated water, and a few secret flavorings to universal distribution. To the jetties of Rangoon, to the sands of the Sahara, and ultimately to outer space itself it went. And in an industry of larger-than-life leaders, such as Woodruff and Candler, it was the individualistic Sledge who, to borrow from an encomium extended Georgia statesman Benjamin Harvey Hill, "by the sheer force of his intellect and personality ruled."

Coca-Cola people having the temerity to question the cost and rationale for Sledge's advertising initiatives routinely came to regret such impertinence. On such occasions the crusty Sledge would remind them, "There can be only one advertising manager." At the same time he was famous for his carefully crafted, diplomatic letters to the family of more than 1,000 franchised bottlers whenever they did air misgivings. These essay-length replies patiently and persuasively explained the rationale for frequency, variety, or types of media employed.[7]

Sledge's capacity to mobilize the bottler body behind the advertising was legendary, remembers Frank Barron of the Rome Coca-Cola Bottling Company. A fifteen-year-old at the time of The Coca-Cola Company/Coca-Cola Bottler 1947 convention in Atlantic City—the first since before World War II—the bottler-to-be was introduced to the advertising manager in an excitement-charged atmosphere. It was the Coca-Cola equivalent of V-E Day; sugar rationing had gone the way of women's painted-on hose and K-rations.[8]

For the first time, the hosts treated the franchisee-guests to a Broadway-style production replete with original music. "Delony gave a great presentation—he was so witty and persuasive," says Barron. "Mr. Sledge was a small man— completely bald, with piercing eagle eyes that cut right through you," he reminisces, a half-century later still in awe of the advertising leader.[9]

Sledge's wit often turned to irreverence. When a fellow officer unveiled what he considered a red-hot advertising idea, a hush fell over the management cadre gathered. With all eyes on the advertising director, Sledge paused and emitted an unmistakable Bronx cheer. No further discussion of the initiative ensued.[10]

But Sledge knew when to put frivolity aside. "When Delony went to see the agency or the networks in New York, he was strictly business—no cocktail drinking, no dining at

'21', no big expense accounts; just conduct business and exit," recalls Atlanta bottler Arthur Montgomery. Always paying attention to the details of his business is how Coca-Cola Company trademark attorney Julius R. Lunsford Jr. recalls the advertising director, as well. The attorney relates that once during the late 1930s he was returning to Atlanta with Sledge and company president Arthur A. Acklin. The latter chided Sledge for not being able to come up with an important piece of information from his ad agency sessions that day. Sledge abruptly disembarked in Philadelphia, returning to New York to get the answer. If the man was not one to suffer fools gladly, he certainly was not willing to risk being one himself. He was, according to *Advertising Age*, "a man who fought a running war with the advertising business, an industry he loves, because it never quite measures up to his image of what it should be."[11]

America's Drink

Much has been written about the so called "cola wars" between America's leading soft drink manufacturers and the large role advertising plays in the constant skirmishes. In a volume titled *The Cola Wars*, one of the industry's lead players ascribes to Coca-Cola's principal competitor a role as "key shapers of the American character." Advertising "harnessed the power of these bonds, elevating the drinks—and the companies—into sovereign symbols of American enterprise...."[12]

Such rhetoric, said *Advertising Age* in 1963, drew from Delony Sledge the comment that it "makes me sick." It was

---

only Coca-Cola, Sledge declared, that deserved designation as "America's Drink."[13]

During the years of the Cold War, a Coke vice-president was quoted to the effect that if those in other nations confused the product with the U.S.A. itself, "perhaps we shouldn't argue" with the impression. More basic was the ads' effort to associate the product with the simple pleasures of living. That was done through appeals to pause, smile, work, shop, and play refreshed. The settings were small town main streets and bustling, at work large cities.[14]

Earlier ad subjects glorified Southern—and, later, American—womanhood. "There is nothing so suggestive of Coca-Cola than a beautiful, sweet, wholesome womanly woman." As Sledge arrived on the scene, the company was featuring popular Hollywood stars like Claudette Colbert, Joan Crawford, Clark Gable, and Don Ameche. And in those Depression years, among the affordable pleasures were Coca-Cola and the movies.[15]

A few years later, Coke enlisted in the war effort. Themes were: "Universal Symbol of the American Way of Life," "As American as Independence Day," and "Coca-Cola Helps Show the World the Friendliness of American Ways." And as the bottler network brought the product "Within an Arm's Length of Desire," Coke could make its claim, "Host to Thirsty Main Street." Artists Norman Rockwell and Haddon Sundblom—the latter with his pervasive Santa Claus enjoying the drink—worked their magic.[16]

THE COCA-COLA COMPANY HAD ITS OWN CUSTOMERS, those who were served by the Fountain Division—including everyone from the mom-and-pop soda fountain to McDonald's. The Bottler Sales Development, on the other hand, was charged with boosting syrup sales to the franchised bottlers. Bottler sales had just one kind of customer, the ones who bottled and distributed the six-and-one-half ounce containers carrying one ounce of syrup mixed with carbonated water.

With Sledge, added emphasis was placed upon expanding bottler sales, especially in light of increased competition from other soft drink corporations. The company people sold their latest advertising campaign and promotions with renewed zeal. There were more incentives to get bottlers to introduce new products or new packages: new radio and television spots and a steady stream of sales promotions designed to create a flurry of activity at the point-of-sale. For example, Fountain Sales had their "Nothing Beatsa Coke and Pizza" campaign, while Bottler Sales once rode with a consumer contest offering a free ocean voyage, "Cook's Cruise with Coke."[17]

Up through the 1950s, company folks joined Delony Sledge and his predecessors in putting on "the safari," a traveling road show brought to bottlers in major cities. Show business figures were featured in the advertising to help sell the syrup—the Company's sole product. Along the way the Broadway-style musical, *Look to the Leader*, dazzled bottlers at the company's mammoth seventy-fifth anniversary celebration in Miami Beach. So impressed were the bottlers that they besieged company personnel to come to a score of locations across the country with the gala "so my route salesmen and their wives can see this see this!" And The Coca-Cola Company complied. Bottlers often got what they wanted.[18]

However, one subject often left them frustrated and suspicious. It was "The Cooperative Advertising Program," which they complained became a nightmare when television costs were shared between the company and the bottlers in television "co-ops." The old contractual nickel-a-gallon advertising allowance no longer cut it in a world increasingly influenced through the medium of television. Also, the sheer expense of all this media exposure was staggering, unlike in the old days when a combination of a little local radio and print — augmented by network radio and magazine exposure handled through the company — more than sufficed. Further, bottlers whose territories had the high per-capita consumption figures would split costs, sixty percent of their dollars with the company providing forty percent. Yet the low per-capita bottlers would have to put up as little as forty percent.[19]

The bottlers knew full well the power of saturation advertising. But the creative product — the ads themselves — had to convince the bottlers that their hard-earned dollars were being well spent. So, quarter after quarter, year after year, Delony Sledge had to scramble to outperform the other guy, creatively speaking. And on one occasion, it meant casting loose the D'Arcy agency, who for decades had served the Coca-Cola business so well.[20]

It was Sledge's (and the ad agency's) handiwork that did the heavy-lifting with the bottler body. If the themes were not memorable or a bit off target, Sledge — or the district reps and managers — heard about it from hundreds of bottlers. "Man, my wife can't stand that blonde girl who does the singin'," a bottler might complain. But if the creative was outstanding — "The Pause that Refreshes," "Sixty million times a day," or "It's the Real Thing" — there was a real enthusiasm in the selling.[21]

In all, the bottlers respected Sledge—his wit and intelligence and his practice of "telling it like it is." Seldom was he backed down when the subject was advertising; he always had voluminous market research and ad subject pre-testing close at hand. For example, when The Coca-Cola Company introduced the "king size"—ten ounces in the South, twelve ounces up North— bottlers responded with, "You just want to sell us more syrup." But the company ad men and women were at the ready: "All our research tells us the consumer—especially the family purchasing agent [the housewife]—wants a larger size."[22]

MANY CONSIDER THE STORY OF TWENTIETH-CENTURY advertising the story of Coca-Cola. Testimony to the effectiveness of Coke's advertising is the rate at which the product is sold, and guiding that effort is the disciplined and thoughtful application of sound techniques and savvy marketing. It's the Coca-Cola way, and the totality of it bears the imprint of ad genius Delony Sledge. As former company chairman J. Paul Austin responded when asked to explain an advertising decision to a vocal audience of franchised bottlers, "I must defer to our wonderful Mr. Sledge on that one."[23]

Just a short time before Sledge's birth, Coca-Cola had placed its first outdoor advertising message—a painted wall in what became the Barron family's domain, Cartersville, Georgia. Initially, most bottlers plotted their own course in advertising, designing, and placing their own creations, some even making outrageous health claims not unlike the flourishing patent medicine businessmen of the day.[24]

Ushering in a new era a couple of decades later, however, was something called the Standardization Committee. And its impact in terms of a unified approach to package design, advertising, and a host of other vital areas was tremendous. So, behind leaders like Sledge; his predecessor, Price Gilbert; and the great conceptualizer of Coca-Cola advertising, D'Arcy agency mogul Archie Lee, the enterprise righted its ship.[25]

Up until this point, Coke was advertised mainly in daily newspapers and national magazines, claiming only to be "delicious and refreshing." But by the 1930s, radio, and especially network radio, was becoming a prime venue for popularizing Coke's fizzy essence. The first paid network radio broadcast was beamed across America, sponsored by Coca-Cola, as was the first network television show. And as much as Sledge admired the medium of print—especially in the form of tasteful four-color magazine subjects—he successfully steered the course of Coke's involvement with electronic media. By 1963, the clear majority of Sledge's budget was riding on radio and television.[26]

The accent in these ads was on people enjoying real-life situations while consuming a wholesome refreshment. Any personalities used in the ads had to be as wholesome as the beverage. More than one entertainer was shown the door when they failed to measure up to Sledge's exacting moral code and his highly developed sense of propriety.[27]

For those and other reasons, some were quick to label Delony Sledge an elitist. This much was clear: he tended toward support of a meritocracy, just as he favored a republican form of government, as opposed to one so democratic it slid toward mobocracy. His oft-repeated creed was something he himself was said to have composed, "The True Republican," perhaps inspired by a nineteenth-century essay, "The True Gentleman," committed to memory as part of his college fraternity initiation. (Sledge's model gentleman would never "flatter wealth, cringe before power, or boast of his possessions or achievements.") Family and family connections—and tradition and authority—counted to E. Delony Sledge.[28]

Just as he had with his own life, Sledge had a credo to guide him in his advertising duties. "WHAT CONSTITUTES A GOOD ADVERTISEMENT: AIDA, OR A.I.D.A.—A FOR ATTENTION, attract favorable attention for the product; I FOR INTEREST—having caught the customer's eye, arouse interest; D FOR DESIRE—do this with well-chosen words, appealing illustrations, skillfully composed, shrewdly placed advertisements; A FOR ACTION!—having gained universal distribution, ask for the order."[29]

Simple? In its fundamental concept, yes, but powerfully targeted in execution. For example, desirable consequences were highlighted in a column written by E. B. Weiss for *Printer's Ink* on 28 November 1952. The piece still rings true when the author explains why "I Like Coke":

1. Here is one large advertiser who has never exaggerated; never displayed poor taste; never featured cheesecake, schmalz or falsies; I say never. 2. Coca-Cola can never be accused of ants-in-the-pants advertising...has stuck with its basic advertising themes...and its basic media year after year. Coca-Cola has also been prompt to take advantage of new advertising techniques...and has stuck with advertising through thick and thin....Coca-Cola has been a credit to advertising...and that is why advertising has done a creditable job for Coke.[30]

The year 1964 saw Delony Sledge operating much as he had for thirty-one years in the business that was his life. But outside the Coca-Cola compound on North Avenue, the times were changing.

In 1964 and 1965, some famous figures departed the scene, among them: Winston Churchill, Herbert Hoover, Albert Schweitzer, World War I hero Alvin York, and CBS News' patron saint, Edward R. Murrow. A plot was uncovered to blow up the Statue of Liberty, the Liberty Bell, and the Washington Monument. All over the country—and not just in the South—there were sit-ins and riots, the largest of the latter in the Watts section of Los Angeles. The Summerhill riots soon would come to Atlanta.[31]

FBI director J. Edgar Hoover called Martin Luther King Jr. the "most notorious liar in the country." Soon after the characterization, King was honored in his hometown of Atlanta upon his becoming a Nobel Peace Prize laureate. The Coca-Cola Company's Woodruff and Austin saw to it that Atlanta's predominantly white business community made an appropriate response.[32]

Meanwhile, Marshall McLuhan changed thinking about the nature and shape of mass communications by writing *Understanding Media.* Pop art was the rage, employing blinding color to complement its savage satirization of contemporary values for living in twentieth-century America. Societal change was rife, sweeping the venerable soft drink business along with it.[33]

Even Coca-Cola, who until 1955 had marketed just one product in just one size—the familiar six-and-one-half ounce returnable bottle—began to diversify their product mix. The Coca-Cola Company acquired Minute Maid with its line of citrus products and Duncan Foods, which marketed instant tea and coffee, some of it in the form of house brands for large retailers. All were erstwhile competitors in the battle to slake consumers' thirsts.[34]

The soft drink business's number-two company had a strategy, said a public relations agent, of portraying the industry leader as a kind of fussy Southern dowager who was about to suffer an undignified pratfall. The drinkers of the number-two entity's product claimed to be turned off by "the old guy." Some of the bottlers began to have doubts, as well, taking advertising matters into their own hands. "I couldn't get Delony to recognize the youth market and its consumer potential," remembers Atlanta bottler Arthur Montgomery. "So I finally just recorded my own rock & roll commercials in a local studio and aired them."[35]

But the bottlers as a whole, including Montgomery, still knew, trusted, and swore by the doughty ad man who was not to "go gently into that quiet night" known as retirement. "I don't think Delony had much of a social life," says Montgomery, "but as conservative and proper as he was, he was great to work with when the going got tough."[36]

Shortly before the tolling of mandatory retirement for Sledge, Coke Chairman J. Paul Austin handed the thirty-two-year advertising veteran an especially challenging assignment, recalls Montgomery, who was paired with him to represent the bottlers' interests. Atlanta's black ministers were poised to target Coca-Cola for discrimination in the hiring and promotion of black employees in the city. It was 1964, and the Atlanta mayor was bent on bringing big-time sports and economic growth to the city. President Lyndon Johnson was pushing civil rights legislation through Congress. There was no room for racial disharmony in the mix.[37]

Without question, the Southern Christian Leadership Conference had the soft drink giant on its hit list. Reverend Joseph E. Lowery, who retired as president of the SCLC in 1997, and other black leaders were after the city's most visible institu-tion. "We had not a single black in even a middle manage-ment position," concedes Montgomery, "and those ministers were flat angry."[38]

So here were two sons of the South, Sledge and Montgomery, who had known nothing but a racially segregated society, admitting discrimination and seeking an accommodation. Coincident with the talks was official recognition of blacks as prime consumers of the beverage — a market segment comprising twelve percent of the nation's population. The company subsequently stepped up its marketing efforts toward this heretofore underserved audience. This, at a time when an African bottler visiting The Coca-Cola Company's headquarters could not even be lodged at a first-class hostelry.[39]

Arthur Montgomery remembers, "Delony acquitted himself with dignity and represented the business with great distinction; I hope the same could be said of me. I was proud of what was accomplished, and I hired the first black manager at my company. His name was Paul E. X. Brown, and he did a fine job for us. The Company soon followed suit." Bottler attitudes about black Americans changed. In the same year as Sledge's and Montgomery's pioneering accomplishment, a reigning patriarch among the bottler clans, Albert M. Biedenharn of San Antonio, asked this writer rhetorically, "Don't you think one hundred years is long enough to make 'em wait?"[40]

Hardly missing a beat after the successful rapprochement, the redoubtable E. Delony Sledge orchestrated the memorable

"Things Go Better With Coke" campaign. It was a memorable one, that campaign in the final months of the era of Sledge. In race relations, things went better for Coke, as well.[41]

AN AD AGENCY CREATIVE MAN, BILL BACKER FORMED a working arrangement with Sledge yielding great benefits for the business. Backer was one of several agency types Sledge had mentored through his career's three decades. In his book, *The Care and Feeding of Ideas*, Backer paints a compelling portrait of Sledge and "devotes interminable space to that one ad," says one associate. The reference is to "I'd Like to Teach the World to Sing (In Perfect Harmony)," performed on an Italian hillside by hundreds of "bright-eyed, fresh scrubbed youths of every color and nationality" to emphasize the international appeal of Coke and the brotherhood of humankind.[42]

While this particular blockbuster came after Sledge's low-key exit in 1965, it was he—with the help of Backer and others—who pioneered with "Things Go Better With Coke" and set the scene for the mountaintop experience. This latter commercial is Arthur Montgomery's favorite and that of countless other of his fellow bottlers. The author observes, "Most people are loyal to themselves or their jobs first. Delony's loyalties lay to the brand first." Backer recalls that as a new man on the account he once tried his hand at describing in writing the taste of "Atlanta holy water" for the ad director. After the monologue was read to him, Sledge "sat for what seemed forever" and then slowly, carefully spoke:

William Faulkner tried to describe this product. So did James Dickey. So have many of your peers over the years. I don't think the words exist. What suffices for me is for you to understand that the taste of Coca-Cola is the greatest taste ever invented by man — or God, either, for that matter.[43]

With a classical allusion Sledge would have admired, Backer concluded, "It was his Saint Crispin's Day speech for any new troops on the account." Sounding like a son reflecting on the wisdom of a deceased father whom he misses, the executive says now he often thinks while consuming the beverage, "Y' know something, the old man was right."[44]

Endnotes

1 James M. Wimberly, interview by author, Atlanta, Georgia, 22 February 1997.

2 Frederick Allen, *Secret Formula: How Brilliant Marketing and Relentless Salesmanship Made Coca-Cola the Best Known Product in the World* (New York: HarperBusiness, 1994) 206-211.

3 John F. Stegeman, *These Men She Gave: A Civil War Diary of Athens, Georgia* (Athens: University of Georgia Press, 1964) 7-9, 15-17; Frances Taliaferro Thomas, *A Portrait of Historic Athens and Clarke County* (Athens: University of Georgia Press, 1992) 258.

4 Indeed, many of Atlanta's leaders through the years hailed from the less-populous areas of the state, among them: Asa G. Candler came to the city from Villa Rica, Georgia — with just $1.75 on his person, it is said — where he had worked as a pharmacist's apprentice. Ivan Allen Sr., first a typewriter salesman and later the consummate civic booster and father of Mayor Ivan Allen Jr., came from Dalton. James B. Williams, until recently CEO of SunTrust Banks, grew up near Rossville on the Tennessee-Georgia line. The Coca-Cola Company General Counsel Pope F. Brock was provided his first suit of clothes and pair of shoes from his neighbors in the Gum Log settlement near Toccoa before setting off to the University of Georgia. See Allen, *Secret Formula*, 32; Ivan Allen Sr., *The Atlanta Spirit: Altitude + Attitude* (Atlanta: n.p., 1916); and *Stephens County, Georgia, and its People, volume 1* (Toccoa GA: Stephens County Historical Society, 1996) 4, 15, 17.

5 The Coca-Cola Company Archives, Atlanta, Georgia.

6 *Advertising Age*, 26 August 1963.

7 Recollection of the author.

8 Frank W. Barron, interview by author, Rome, Georgia, 12 March 1997.

9 Ibid.

10 The advertising director's sense of humor, for the most part, was appreciated by his associates. When this author, then a junior ad exec at the company, experienced a painful rejection of a budget

proposal, he sulked in his office late into the evening. Sledge made a point of marching by the man's office and, gazing resolutely ahead, remarked, "Cheatham, surrounded by his friends."

[11] Arthur L. Montgomery, interview by author, 11 April 1997; Julius R. Lunsford Jr., esq., letter to the author, 25 March 1997; *Advertising Age*, 23 August 1963.

The frugal Sledge—never one to be profligate with company funds or his own—had a practice of taking holiday greeting cards sent, signing his own name on same and returning them to well-wishers.

[12] L. C. Louis and Harvey Z. Yazijian, *The Cola Wars* (New York: The Everest House, 1980) 101-103.

[13] *Advertising Age*, 23 August 1963.

[14] Louis and Yazijian, 101-103.

[15] Advertisements in The Coca-Cola Company Archives, including *Saturday Evening Post*, 23 October 1933.

[16] Ibid.; Allen, *Secret Formula*.

[17] Bottler sales meeting script, Spring 1964; recollection of the author.

[18] Recording of *Look to the Leader*.

[19] Barron interview.

[20] Allen, *Secret Formula*, 306-307.

[21] Barron interview.

[22] John C. Brown, interview by author, Seattle, Washington, November 1989.

[23] Karen W. King, Associate Professor, University of Georgia College of Journalism and Mass Communications, interview by author, 17 March 1997; recollection of author.

[24] "Earliest Coca-Cola Wall Sign Uncovered in Georgia," *Binghamton (N.Y.) Press and Sun Bulletin*, 4 June 1989; Mark Pendergast, *For God, Country, and Coca-Cola* (New York: Scribners, 1993).

[25] Lillian Hooper Hardison, "Coca-Cola Bottling Plants: The Preservation of Standardized Early Twentieth Century Commercial Property" (master's thesis, University of Georgia, 1994).

[26] The Coca-Cola Company Archives.

[27] Richard D. Harvey, interview by author, Seattle, Washington, Winter 1990.

[28] Joanne Newman, The Coca-Cola Company Archives, interview by author, Atlanta, Georgia, 7 September 1993.

[29] The Coca-Cola Company Archives.

[30] E. B. Weiss, *Printer's Ink*, 28 November 1952.

[31] "Obituaries 1964," *Encyclopedia Britannica Year Book* (New York: Encyclopedia Britannica, 1964); "Civil Rights," *Encyclopedia Britannica Year Book* (New York: Encyclopedia Britannica, 1965); Ivan Allen Jr. with Paul Hemphill, *Mayor: Notes on the Sixties* (New York: Simon and Schuster, 1971).

[32] Allen, *Mayor.*

[33] Marshall McLuhan, *Understanding Media: The Extensions of Man* (New York: McGraw-Hill, 1964).

[34] 1963 and 1964 Annual Reports, The Coca-Cola Company.

[35] George Bevil, interview by author, Atlanta, Georgia, Winter 1964; Montgomery interview.

[36] Montgomery interview.

[37] "Civil Rights," *Encyclopedia Britannica Year Book* (New York: Encyclopedia Britannica, 1965).

[38] Montgomery interview.

[39] The Coca-Cola Company Archives.

[40] Montgomery interview; Albert M. Biedenharn, conversation with the author, 1964.

[41] Ibid.

[42] Ibid.

[43] Ibid., 235-237.

[44] Ibid.

10

GREAT LEADERS, GREAT FOUNDATIONS, GREAT COMMUNITIES

In many ways, the story of the Coca-Cola bottling business in Georgia—and indeed nationally and internationally—has been the story of the twentieth century. From the founding of the parent entity in 1886 and the start-up of what became the Atlanta Coca-Cola Bottling Company in 1900, the Coca-Cola bottling business has been a mighty engine of growth helping to power the country and the region. And in the vanguard of that expansion and prosperity has been the state of Georgia.[1]

Thurman Sensing of the Southern States Industrial Council was a spokesman for an ardent brand of advocacy for a prosperous Southland. At mid-century, through the medium of his newspaper columns, Sensing proclaimed—endlessly, some said—"The second half of the twentieth century belongs to the South." The region had not enjoyed such prospects after the Civil War; despair and poverty were everywhere. By 1938, amid the Great Depression, President Franklin Delano Roosevelt would declare the section "the nation's number one economic problem" and commissioned the National Emergency Board to document that statement and its consequences.

Sixty years later the Southern Regional Education Board revisited the report for the President, and the South's transformation was found to be dramatic. The percentage of adults with high school degrees had risen from nineteen to seventy-nine; the percentage of adults with college degrees up from four to twenty-one; and the percentage of the national average income had gone from fifty-two to ninety-two. Georgia's average income was at ninety-four percent.

The number of medical colleges in the South, twenty in 1938, was at forty-five; and cases of malaria, at an estimated two million in the Depression era, had dropped to a solitary one in 1998. The twenty-eight percent of Americans living in the fifteen Southern states had finally achieved parity with the remainder of the nation: twenty-eight percent of the nation's people, twenty-eight percent of the country's bank deposits— rising from only eleven percent in the first year of Roosevelt's second term.[2]

GREAT LEADERS

The role of Coca-Cola men and women in a Southern renaissance mirrored the successful transformation of the region. And in that, three factors have been most apparent: great leaders, great foundations, and great communities.

For the Coca-Cola part of this equation, M. Douglas Ivester offers illumination about some of his company's towering leaders, about whom much already has been written. In The Coca-Cola Company's 1997 *Annual Report*, the share-owners letter from Ivester, chairman of the board of directors and chief executive officer, states that:

[T]hose who came before us blazed a trail with their vision, their imagination, their creativity and their dedication....But their legacy is more than might appear from a first glance at their achievements. Among those pioneers, none stood taller in creating value for our shareholders than Roberto C. Goizueta, who led your Company for 16 years as chairman of our board of directors and chief executive officer. He regarded our mission, creating value for you over time, as paramount.... First came the creator of Coca-Cola, John Pemberton, 113 years ago. Later came Asa Candler, the originator of twentieth-century Coca-Cola marketing; Robert Woodruff, for 60 years the architect of our Company's success and father of our international expansion; and many thousands more Coca-Cola men and women, less famous but no less crucial in their pioneering efforts.[3]

In the pantheon of the greats of Coca-Cola business, these, mentioned by Ivester, and many others shared a vision of what that enterprise was, is, and could become. Indeed they were visionaries — but not as mere dreamers. They believed, and practiced, something very near to that credo expressed by the protagonist of a 1961 novel by Frank C. Norris. Speaking the lines is a character, Jay Candless, a dynamic Southerner who has risen to a position of great influence and wealth in the world of refreshment and high finance:

Men create wealth, I believe, by the projection of their personalities on the world....And most of the successful ones do so, I also believe, by the grace of their perception of just two things: product and persuasion. A lucky line of ballyhoo can sell a certain amount of brummagem, and a certain amount of an honorable service can be merchandised even by unskillful promotion. But the combination of a fine commodity to sell and an energetic and persuasive means of selling it is the goal of an effective organization. That is the sublime situation, the one for which it is worth working hardest. And of course it is a great deal more fun that way. I had all this pretty much figured out, even before the end of the first year that I was with the company.[4]

The Jay Candless character in so many admirable respects resembles Robert W. Woodruff that it is well-nigh impossible to conclude that the author was constructing his yarn around anyone other than the charismatic Georgian. For example, the depth of Candless's dedication to his native city, state, and region is rivaled only by his determination to have the enterprise succeed on a global scale.

Indeed, the man Robert Woodruff picked to carry on his legacy—which included the creation of wealth and the proper use of it—was Roberto C. Goizueta, the CEO at The Coca-Cola Company who was chosen by *Time* as one of the 100 most influential "builders and titans" of the century. His contribution, said the magazine, stemmed from his being "an avid disciple of the idea of economic value creation," something his mentor, Woodruff, no doubt imparted to his own disciple in the business.[5]

Still, of all the names, four other notable individuals come quickly to mind as leaders in the Coca-Cola business, principally because they were so typically the products of the best of their times. All would have been in perfect consonance with what Norris's character professed. They were: W. C. Bradley of Columbus, outside director and from 1919 to 1939 chairman of the board; Harrison Jones of Atlanta, first an officer of the company and then its chairman from 1942 to 1952; Veazey Rainwater, a native of Greene County, Georgia, who served with Joseph B. Whitehead and then went over to the company with its in-house "parent bottler" (and who later became a successful franchised bottler himself); and Harold Hirsch, general counsel, who had wielded tremendous influence over the affairs of the Coca-Cola business, at times representing the legal interests of both the parent and its franchisees.[6]

The four great leaders—Bradley, Jones, Hirsch, and Rainwater—had at least two things in common. Each operated within the broad parameters of a special relationship with Robert W. Woodruff, becoming in many ways Woodruff's alter ego. Moreover, each assumed a distinctive persona as "the bottler's friend" and was perceived by the bottlers as such.

W. C. BRADLEY

If Dr. Pemberton was "the originator" (adapting Ivester's phrase), then W. C. Bradley could be called "the enabler." It was he who made it possible for Ernest Woodruff (the president of Trust Company of Georgia, a onetime Columbus resident, and a onetime neighbor of Bradley's) to form a syndicate to acquire The Coca-Cola Company in 1919 from Asa G. Candler for $25 million dollars—at that time the largest financial transaction ever in the South. Some have said that Bradley "loaned the money" to Ernest Woodruff for the acquisition. When a young associate asked Joseph W. Jones, perhaps Robert W. Woodruff's most trusted and longest-serving retainer, if that in fact had been the case, Jones reported to the associate days later: "He said he might have, he might have."[7]

Whatever the case, Bradley served as chairman of the board until 1939 and chairman of the advisory committee until 1946. He was Robert Woodruff's confidant and mentor, and it was the younger Woodruff's custom to address Bradley in correspondence as, "My Dear Uncle Will."[8]

The Columbus man was eighteen years old when Candler set up for business as "The Coca-Cola Company." It was he — a universally respected leader — "who kept the grass roots intact" and enjoyed the bottlers' complete confidence, says Bradley's grandson, William Bradley Turner. When the company came on lean years as a result of signing on to a sugar contract at what became a disastrous price level (thirty cents per pound, after the commodity's price tumbled to five cents), Bradley came up with $4 million of his own money to see the firm through the crisis.[9]

As might be said of the bottlers profiled in earlier chapters, the influence of the man who presided over the board of directors during most of the first half of the twentieth century was felt most keenly in his home base of Columbus, but it radiated outward into many spheres of activity and influence throughout the South and nation. Grandson William B. Turner — who like his father, D. Abbott Turner, served many years on the company's board of directors — acknowledges that W. C. Bradley indeed was "the biggest banker, warehouseman, farmer, and cotton manufacturer" of his day in the Chattahoochee Valley. Bradley served as chairman, president, or board member of at least eighteen corporations and was president of Columbus Bank and Trust.[10]

The Bradley empire and its gentle giant of a leader could be viewed from the Chattahoochee River, whose waters his steamship fleet plied. Upon his death *The Columbus Ledger-Enquirer* labeled him "the biggest river man of his generation." Starting as a clerk, the man bought out the cotton factoring firm for which he worked, added a wholesale grocery operation, and began to manufacture high-grade fertilizer for use by cotton farmers. He became chairman of The Coca-Cola Company and the Central of Georgia Railroad, as well.[11]

The company is still located at its original 1899 location in the historic district of Columbus. On the premises are located the corporate offices, the W. C. Bradley Company Museum, and the D. A. Turner Memorial Chapel, the latter a gift of the company's employees to shareholders during the firm's centennial celebration in 1995. It is from this very spot that the Bradley-Turner Foundation, founded in 1943, mounted a challenge to forge a renaissance for the old river city. The results of this "Columbus Challenge" have firmly established W. C. Bradley as a hero.[12]

A measure of Bradley's stature and influence for good was offered recently by his grandson, William Bradley Turner. "When the crash came and everything in this section was in a bad way, it was he who almost single-handedly kept the cotton mills open and saw to it workers held on to their jobs." And while Bradley in fact was the "Empire Builder" spoken of in a local newspaper headline upon his death, it was also true, as noted in yet another front-page headline, that "Friendliness Marked W. C. Bradley's Life." He had about him a kind of fundamental simplicity, humility, and integrity.[13]

Today at the W. C. Bradley Company, there is a manager in charge of relations with "stakeholders" — those constituencies who share an interest in what happens at the company and whose lives and fortunes in some way are affected by the company and by its philanthropic arm, the Bradley-Turner Foundation, which ranks in the top tier of assets in the state of Georgia.[14]

One of Georgia's outstanding bankers and business executives is James M. Blanchard of Columbus. Blanchard is chief executive officer of Synovus Financial Corporation, and he has known the Bradley family since birth. His assessment of Bradley-Turner and the W. C. Bradley Company is impressive: "The Bradley-Turner Foundation to Columbus has been every bit as significant, if not more so, than the Woodruff Foundation to Atlanta. I can't imagine a modern-day, growing, progressive Columbus without their influence and support." It should be noted that people living in the hometowns of the bottlers featured in this book typically express the same kind of esteem and affection for *their* bottler.[15]

Blanchard adds, "The W. C. Bradley Family today — including the Turner family, Butler family and Corn family — are great examples of Christian principles in real life. They live the values that others can aspire to live. They are a wonderful source of inspiration for those who know them and see them up close."[16]

These values are apparent from the "Columbus Challenge." The magazine *Georgia Trend*, in its June 1998 edition, ran a feature revealing the inner workings behind the transformation of the proud old river city. Columbus Mayor Bobby Peters attributes the success of the $86.4 million fund-rasing challenge to the coming together of foundations, the private sector, the public at large, and a host of other leaders — among them state and federal elected and non-elected officials, city council members, and educators. It was the challenge for renewal from Bradley-Turner—to the tune of $20 million, later supplemented by another $5 million—that served as the catalyst for contributions from all sectors of Columbus society. Citizens exceeded their $25 million target by $3.4 million. Other funds, including $17 million for a Performing Arts Center to be known as RiverCenter, came by the initiation of Georgia Governor Zell Miller.[17]

The $86.4 million is slated for several desired civic improvements, a number related to the arts. Included are the Columbus Museum, Springer Opera House, Woodruff Museum of Civil War Naval History, Columbus Symphony, The Coca-Cola Space Science Center, Liberty Theater, and Historic Columbus Foundation. The handsome Riverwalk, says Peggy Theus of the Bradley-Turner Foundation, will make the Chattahoochee River the front door to the city rather than an embarrassment to hide from view. The river, which powered the original growth of Columbus during the late-nineteenth century, of course happens to be the same transportation artery that served W. C. Bradley and his commercial pursuits.[18]

The 1996 Olympics played a vital role, as well, in the revival along the Chattahoochee. The Olympic softball venture came to Columbus, fostering more growth and a proliferation of major sporting events. In a park to be located along the river, plans call for structured tributes to Pemberton and Robert W. Woodruff as well as for Bradley, who is to be represented by a water-powered turbine that will power a model of one of Bradley's steamboats. That somehow seems appropriate, given the fact that he—and what he contributed in his lifetime and through his family—furnished so much of the power, resolve, and vision that has brought his city and region such prominence in the twentieth century.[19]

Robert W. Woodruff, mentored and championed his entire life by Bradley, perhaps best summarized the contributions of the great leader from Columbus. In a tribute to Bradley on the fiftieth anniversary of his company, he likened his impact to that of Henry W. Grady, whom Woodruff proceeded to quote: "It is a privilege to have had a part in the uplifting and upbuilding of the prostrate and bleeding South" after the Civil War. Of course, anyone who knew the longtime board chairman also knew Bradley would never claim such a distinction or a comparison, true in many ways though it was.[20]

A 1960 column by Latimer Watson in the *Columbus Ledger* provides additional insight into Bradley's life and legacy. It seems that the columnist, who earlier that year had written a book review of E. J. Kahn's *The Big Drink*, began to receive all kinds of telephone calls from readers about the review and The Coca-Cola Company's Columbus connection. There had been a reference to how Bradley had stepped in to "save" The Coca-Cola Company after the sugar incident. Watson relates that her readers kept asking, "Why didn't Mr. Bradley insist that he be given credit?" Or, "Why would a man like Mr. Bradley sit back and let his name be left entirely out of the Coca-Cola story?" She then tells of how one small incident she witnessed explained so much about Bradley's character and humility—and why he may have eschewed any credit or acclaim for his role in the business's affairs. It seems that a large crowd of Columbusites had gathered to honor the man by naming a new theater for him. Called upon for remarks at the ceremony, he rose and offered a tremulous salutation— half audible—consisting of something like, "My friends...."

Then, hands shaking, Bradley turned beet red and sat down.[21]

Watson recounts, "There was a second of silence, then the house went wild. The most polished speech in the world couldn't have touched that audience as that did. Mr. Bradley had been almost a legendary figure, a name to most of them. Now he was home folks and they loved it and him." The columnist concludes with this measure of the man and his contribution: "Remembering that evening, it is easy to understand how he would let go uncontested his part in saving Coca-Cola. . . ."[22]

How fortunate were his neighbors in Columbus and his friends with The Coca-Cola Company to have had a man like that, a man "with empires in his purpose and new eras in his brains." [23]

HARRISON JONES

It's the early 1940s and a contingent from Atlanta's Piedmont Driving Club is on a chartered bus, fortified with strong drink and buoyed by high spirits, crossing the Thomas County line deep in South Georgia. The group—composed of some of Atlanta's and Georgia's leading citizens and business leaders—was in transit to a fishing camp in a remote Homosassa, Florida, location. Former Atlanta Mayor Ivan Allen Jr. has his version of what transpired, one in which broad and humorous strokes bring to life cherished memories of the larger-than-life character that was Harrison Jones. "Before we left the club, early in the morning, Harrison walked in and realized Clark Howell and the others already were enjoying themselves at the bar."[24]

Jones, who very rarely imbibed, confronts the autocratic and imperious publisher of *The Atlanta Constitution*, and insists decorum be maintained. "Clark was president of the club and Harrison was chairman of the board, and you could say we were the most over-represented membership any private club ever had because of those two," says Allen remembering that pair of strong-willed leaders.[25]

The bus was stopped at the Thomas County line by a stereotypical South Georgia sheriff, complete with six-guns and a pair of deputies. The violation was transporting alcohol across the line into a dry county. "Alright, boys, I'll handle this," bellows Jones in stentorian tones. Stretching himself to his full height of six feet, three inches over a 250-pound frame, Jones has Hugh Dorsey Jr. — son of the highly esteemed former Governor Hugh Dorsey of Georgia — accompany him as he greets the sheriff. "This is a group of businessmen from Atlanta, sheriff, and you know that there ain't but two things in Georgia — Joneses and Coca-Cola — and I'm both of them!" Disarmed by the audacity of the Coca-Cola chieftain, the lawman becomes conciliatory and permits the men to proceed on their merry way.[26]

The old timers in the Coca-Cola business remember Harrison Jones as a commanding figure, as indeed he was in this instance. Such a spellbinding orator was he that at the first bottlers convention after World War II in Atlantic City, one Georgia-based bottler called aside his dozen or so managers and issued an injunction: "Boys, I want you to have a good time while you're here and just soak up the enthusiasm this business generates; I'm not gonna call the roll every day while we're here, but whatever you do, boys, don't miss hearing Harrison Jones's speech on the last day!"[27]

Atlantans remember him in similar ways. The legendary editor, Ralph McGill, portrayed Jones as "a steam engine in pants." The other Atlanta editor, James Saxon Childers, remembered walking over to Jones's office in the Healey Building and hearing the charismatic figure's voice—in his normal conversational tone—from outside the open windows of the structure and five stories below. And when William Pressly came to Atlanta from The McCallie School in 1951 to become the founding president of The Westminster Schools, he was in for a rare experience with Jones. In advancing the idea of a high-quality academic power for the Atlanta area, Pressly went first to John A. Sibley, then Robert W. Woodruff, and finally to Harrison Jones. With the approval of that trio, the idea had an excellent chance of success.[28]

As Pressly recalled in a 1997 interview, "Harrison Jones was a character if there ever was one. He would pace back and forth behind his desk and let me sit there about an hour and a half and would tell me about all the people I was going to meet in Atlanta who had children that might come to the school." At this point in Pressly's account it begins to sound very much as though the master salesman was selling himself on the proposition. "He never was critical of anybody. Everything he told me was upbeat. He was really a power-house."[29]

The same kind of leadership style and the Jones flair was evident during his college days at the University of Georgia prior to World War I. David C. Barrow, much revered in Athens, had been designated the new chancellor of the nation's first chartered state university. Immediately upon hearing the glad news, Jones enlisted some other student leaders and commandeered as slick a gig as ever seen in the university town—resplendent in the school's colors, red and black. Off they galloped to the Barrow home and summoned forth the chancellor-to-be. Then the joyful band led by Harrison Jones "initiated" Barrow, sweeping grandly into Costa's soda fountain in the Southern Mutual Building and announcing to the assemblage of students, "Coca-Cola for everyone!"[30]

Aside from being especially dapper and articulate, Arthur Montgomery recalls what was special about Jones: "He could make you laugh; he could make you cry; and he darn sure could inspire you to sell Coca-Cola!" Jim Wimberly, a veteran of the Coca-Cola business, recollected a typical Jones moment. Jones, scheduled to speak to his bottlers, would enter the hall with bowed head and walk slowly, each step measured, his leonine countenance borne down in sober reflection. Then mounting the steps to the stage, Wimberly says Jones would remain portentously poised over the lectern before at last lifting his head dramatically to thunder out these words: "What this business needs is some million-dollar funerals!"[31]

McGill, too, once summed up the package that was Jones: "Harrison Jones was a man of many sides, and all of them were effective. He was a salesman and an executive. He could bellow like the bulls of ancient Bashan or be as gentle as a sister of mercy. He could charm the locks right off a door or stand dignified and firm as Gibraltar." But adding a caveat of sorts, McGill stated, "His oratory was not of the sort calculated to make the clouds seem blue and the flowers prettier than they are." Emphasizing another quality, the great editor reported that "for all his bellowing toughness," the man "weeps easily and is deeply touched by all that troubles his friends and community."[32]

His bottlers were his friends, and in many ways family, as one of Jim Wimberly's stories points up. Wimberly tells of traveling to Montgomery, Alabama, where a tribute was being held in honor of the multi-state Bellingrath bottling empire, its founding fathers, and the son-in-law who at that time ran it, Stanhope Elmore, a man of whom longtime bottler leader Sanders Rowland would say was without doubt the most respected and revered bottler of his day.[33]

Harrison Jones was to be the principal speaker, and the time came for him to launch into his peroration. His magnificent baritone voice soared. "And as surely as 'A' is for Alabama...and as surely as 'B' is for Bellingrath...and as surely as 'C' is Coca-Cola...." Then Jones paused abruptly and gazed at Elmore. "Well, I forgot 'D'; DAMN, Elmore!" Actually, Wimberly may have cleaned up the language in the anecdote, for, as those who grew up with him in the business often commented, profanity—even some involving use of the deity's name in vain—were a staple in Harrison Jones's inspirational flights. Jones could remonstrate with his bottlers, inspire them, and do so with "the greatest combination of classical allusion and passionate profanity you ever heard," remembered a family member of the onetime Corpus Christi, Texas, franchisee. The late Coca-Cola Company officer Ovid R. Davis, as well, was fond of Jones's famed "handkerchief speech," during which the Coca-Cola warrior would brandish the accessory-turned-theatrical prop and exhort as he flailed about the handkerchief with telling rhetorical effect. Bottlers loved him, and it was he to whom they turned when there arose—as there inevitably would—a dispute between franchiser and franchisee.[34]

Through his speeches and as the result of the precepts he espoused, Jones made clear to the bottler body that their fates were intertwined with that of the parent. And that was illustrated quite convincingly in a 1948 speech to bottlers by means of an analogy to parenthood:

> Did it ever occur to you that Coca-Cola, the finished beverage, is a child of a marriage between The Coca-Cola Company and the bottler? It comes from the womb of one and the loins of another. Oh, there is mutuality in this deal. But the only thing that counts to any worthwhile parents, and the only thing that counts here, is offspring, and Coca-Cola is the child, the offspring, of that marriage. Oh, I want everybody to have a grand and glorious opinion of The Coca-Cola Company, and I hope everybody in the world knows about it, and I hope everybody in the community knows about you and your integrity and character and standing as a good citizen. But the millions of people in the world don't give a hoot about who the parents of this child are. They know the child. They believe in the offspring. That is our life; that's our blood, and it's that we must perpetuate. And we must adopt the motto that the one spring that springs eternal is offspring. So, we must have unity. We must have cooperation. We are independent, and we can lick the earth.[35]

Paul Austin was a Coca-Cola chief executive officer, a Harvard-educated lawyer whose delivery and communicational bent led him to explain to industry audiences that he had no desire "to go onto the Chautauqua Circuit." He referred to that traveling American phenomenon, which, beginning in 1904, brought three-to-seven day programs of culture to hundreds of small towns and hamlets. The events featured popular public speakers, such as "the great commoner," William Jennings Bryan, and "the great agnostic," Robert G. Ingersoll, as well as dramas and concerts. The Chautauquas were immensely successful for a time, but they were a form of protracted entertainment the likes of which the cerebral and precise Austin saw to be of scant value to the body of bottlers.[36]

But the Chautauqua style suited Harrison Jones to a tee. He was down to earth—and downright earthy, well-educated and well-read though he was. And, of course, America was built more upon agriculture then and small town ways predominated. As he liked to remind the high-fliers among his bottlers, "I ain't never seen a buzzard fly so high that he didn't have to come down for water."[37]

Too, he could strike some themes in his orations that were profoundly spiritual. After all, he taught the men's Bible class at his Baptist church. (Although Harrison Jones II chuckles that given his propensity for great flights of profanity, "I don't know how he got through it every Sunday.") "I suppose what he did wasn't thought of in that day in terms of what we'd call it today—motivational communication," offers Harrison Jones II. But it worked in his grandfather's day and—in different form—is effective today. In fact, the executive was the first in his industry to utilize what today some call "industrial theater"—dramatized stage presentations driving home points about employing scientific selling, utilizing potent advertising, and the turning loose of properly trained and motivated route salesmen. Slick props and scenery and professional actors dramatized Jones's points. An opinion survey of Georgia CEOs appearing in the March 1998 issue of *Georgia Trend* revealed that 94.4 percent of those questioned felt that the CEO/chairman's highest priority and greatest responsibility was to be "inspiring and lead employees." In Jones's case, executive ability and the rare communicational gift to inspire and motivate simply came in the same package.[38]

Much has been made of the fact that the early bottlers of the product were humble men, some with little in the way of formal education. One author of a work of fiction about the business even had a character rail out at his fellow franchisees, going so far as to call his brethren the dumbest bunch he had ever seen. True, many bottlers previously had been employed in jobs on the lower rungs of the vocational ladder — grocery men, railway express agents, secretaries, and such; Jones himself made reference to their humble status. But no matter their background, they all related to Harrison Jones. And with such a clarion call to the audience, who wouldn't line up on the side of cooperation and unity, hard work and devotion to duty? With Harrison Jones leading the charge, "we can lick the world." The bottlers believed it, just as their leader did.[39]

CHARLES VEAZEY RAINWATER

As the ringleaders of the bottler conventions, Harrison Jones of The Coca-Cola Company and Charles Veazey Rainwater of the bottlers' association were the featured attractions. Rainwater enjoyed the distinction of having the longest continuing service record in the history of the Coca-Cola bottling business, seventy-one years. He helped organize the primary trade organization of the industry, and working with Jones and the bottlers he saw to it that a "Standardization Committee" created consistency in uniform selection, truck design and color, and bottling plant architecture. Considering that Rainwater was trying to get a "choir" of 1,100 bottlers to "sing off the same sheet of music," his harmonizing was no small accomplishment.[40]

At age twenty, Rainwater had gone from part-time to full-time status as secretary to J. B. Whitehead, stayed in Chattanooga for a time in service to J. T. Lupton, and after a few years moved to Atlanta to work for Whitehead. He had first used Athens and Augusta as his base of operations and had scoured the Southern states for likely investors/franchisees. Evidently he was quite successful, for by 1909 he had hosted the first convention for Coca-Cola people. Hundreds of bottlers attended and returned to their plants refreshed and full of zeal for selling the concoction. Such affairs became very popular, with bottlers and company men alike. There were stem-winding speeches from the cheerleading principals and even boxing and wrestling matches with professional contestants to divert attendees. When it came to signing up bottlers and turning them loose on their territories, Rainwater was the master "rainmaker."[41]

While Rainwater may have been an indispensable man for the parent bottler, he was so highly respected by the "actual" bottlers that when Woodruff and his men from the company bought out the Whitehead rights and operated the parent bottler from in-house, Veazey Rainwater moved over as well, becoming the vice president in charge of that operation. After only two years, however, he resolved to become an independent bottler and operate Hygeia Coca-Cola Bottling out of Pensacola, Florida. The bottling company grew to include nine companies and twelve plants. In addition to a strong presence in the Florida city, there were operations in Beaumont and Port Arthur, Texas, as well as in some Georgia cities.[42]

Harold Hirsch was from a prominent Atlanta Jewish family, had played football at the University of Georgia, and for many years was the principal Coca-Cola Company conduit to the university's athletic program. With company money he provided the university football scholarships—when that was legal, insofar as the ruling bodies of collegiate sport were concerned—and he traveled with the team as they sallied forth to defeat Yale and other Eastern powers. Hirsch saw to it, as well, that the athletes obtained jobs with The Coca-Cola Company after graduation. But Hirsch was a strong link to another, non-athletic endeavor at the state university. The school of law, from which he graduated in the first decade of the century, would name its building Hirsch Hall, in his honor, in 1932.[43]

Armed with a law degree, Hirsch first joined the firm of Candler, Thomson, and Hirsch in 1906 and worked on the sale of The Coca-Cola Company by Candler to the Woodruff/Trust Company of Georgia syndicate in 1919. The firm's senior partner was Asa's brother, John S. Candler, who for a time even served on the Georgia Supreme Court while handling the Coca-Cola account. It was Hirsch who brought Harrison Jones, a University of Georgia contemporary, into the Candler firm and then persuaded him in 1919 to go over to the company and reorganize its field sales organization. Hirsch knew a natural salesman when he saw him.[44]

Hirsch's influence on Robert Woodruff was great, and he remained his counsel and mentor for two decades. But his leadership in the early Woodruff years made for a smoother transition from the Candler years. Hirsch's steady hand was especially evident during the bitter company-bottler litigation over the contract in the early 1920s when issues arose as to whether the contract was one in perpetuity and how the fluctuating cost of sugar should be factored when arriving at a price for syrup sold to bottlers. And despite the fact that it made for some uncomfortable times for the lawyer when he actually represented both the company and the bottlers, it was always Hirsch and W. C. Bradley who reconciled the warring clans.[45]

To fully appreciate the influence of a Harold Hirsch—or, for that matter, the Coca-Cola influence upon the University of Georgia—one need only examine those featured at the dedication exercises for Hirsch Hall at the university's school of law on 29 October 1932. It was an all Coca-Cola show. Principal speakers were as follows: Hughes Spalding, who referred to Harrison Jones as "that two-fisted, hard-boiled go-getter who had more sense than any of us," when he quit practicing law and became executive vice president of The Coca-Cola Company; J. J. Spalding, father of Hughes; Alexander C. King, for whom the school's law library was named and who was Spalding's law partner; Marion Smith, president of the Georgia Bar Association; Harold Hirsch, for whom the building was named; and Harrison Jones.[46]

While applying his wisdom and counsel, Hirsch rendered influence for the public weal far beyond the pursuit of its solely business purposes. As the Georgia Bar Association's Marion Smith said:

> There is a lawyer who recognizes that his profession brings him closely in touch with the forces that mold public opinion and control the course of progress, and who recognizes that there is a public duty resting

upon him to use his influence always in behalf of right and justice and social progress. His work is a public service, frequently of more importance than that of holding office, although sometimes the two are combined....When we wish to tell pupils entering these halls the ideal that is held before them, we do so simply, but clearly and completely, by writing the name, Harold Hirsch, above the entrance to the building.[47]

The name stands there today, below the inscription "Iustitia" — Justice. And a foundation in Atlanta bearing the Hirsch name bestows college scholarships upon young Georgians.[48]

None of the foregoing discussion of Hirsch's virtues or the vast extent of his influence is to suggest that his pro bono work — or especially his support of his alma mater — had little relation to his safeguarding of his client's best interests. For example, Governor Huey Long of Louisiana, prior to the 1936 football season, informed Georgia officials there *would* be a game between the Bulldogs and Louisiana State University at Baton Rouge. And on short notice at that. It amounted to a high-handed tactic typical of a governor who would march at the head of his team's band at halftime. Hirsch was then given to understand that if Georgia did not clear its schedule for the game with the Tigers, he could expect imposition of an onerous penny-a-bottle soft drink tax in Long's state. Hirsch accommodated the Louisiana chief executive, and Hirsch's team would suffer a humiliating 47-0 defeat at Baton Rouge.[49]

Three years after the dedication of Hirsch Hall, John Sibley of the Spalding law firm took over the responsibility as counsel to The Coca-Cola Company as well as Woodruff's personal lawyer. Sibley's and Spalding's firm had represented the bottlers in bitterly fought litigation in the early 1920s concerning the issue of whether franchises were granted in perpetuity or were contracts "at will." Only four years later Harold Hirsch was dead. The year was 1939.[50]

In a special tribute to Hirsch, several thousand students gathered for a pep rally on the eve of the Holy Cross-Georgia football game. Hatton Lovejoy, president of the alumni society, reminded them "the greatest friend of Georgia athletics was lost in the death of Harold Hirsch." In a moving tribute to the great legal counsel, Lovejoy said, "His death calls to mind something of the Bible verse referring to the death of a great man in an ancient day: 'A Prince of Israel has fallen today.'"[51]

A Shining, Golden Opportunity

In some ways, one facet of Harrison Jones's and Harold Hirsch's personalities could be highlighted by what some might call "The Andy Roddenbery Story." The young Phi Beta Kappa football star, S. Anderson Roddenbery, was able to attend the University of Georgia only due to the faith in him expressed by great community leaders in his hometown of Macon, Georgia, who awarded to the Lanier High School graduate a scholarship to attend the state's university. When Roddenbery's coaches in Athens observed that the young man had an aptitude for medicine, they urged him to go to medical school. A downcast Roddenbery, the product of a

---

broken home, replied that he had nowhere near the money required for that pursuit.

The coaches advised that he go see Harrison Jones and Harold Hirsch. Roddenbery remembers that an assistant football coach, Ted Twomey, advised him "he had set up the deal" and to "go see Harold Hirsch and he will make the necessary financial arrangements." So, as Roddenbery recalls, "on Saturday afternoon I visited Mr. Hirsch at his modest home at 118 Waverly Way, N.E. He and his wife were listening to the Texaco Opera radio program." Hirsch told Andy, "you have done a lot for Georgia, Andy, and we want to help you." Pausing as the maid brought the pair cold Coca-Cola, Hirsch asked, "Where do you want to go to medical school?" Harvard, replied Roddenberry. And Harvard it was to be.

Hirsch's partner in the funding was Harrison Jones, and Roddenbery went to see Jones—who "filled me with the desire to make something of myself." During a lengthy session in the executive offices, with several people cooling heels outside as Jones did the "inculcating," the Coca-Cola chieftain discussed with the young graduate ways to eradicate hookworm and malaria in South Georgia. "I owe my opportunity to study medicine to the support and generosity of two of the greats of The Company—Harold Hirsch and Harrison Jones", says Roddenbery. What a blessing from God. They asked nothing in return and seemed to glory in my achievements. You can imagine my everlasting appreciation and my loyalty and love of 'Coke.'"

And the rest is history. Roddenbery had a distinguished medical career as a surgeon, establishing a practice in

Columbus and, in time, recruiting and training Delmar Edwards, the first black surgeon in all of South Georgia. In his life of achievement, Andy Roddenbery had no stronger allies in his search for a career of service through the practice of medicine than his friends in the Coca-Cola business, Hirsch and Jones. Their generosity and encouragement made it possible for him—and scores of other young people—to attain, as Thomas Wolfe once wrote, "his chance—to every man, regardless of his birth, his shining golden opportunity—to every man the right to live, to work, to be himself, and to become whatever thing his manhood and his vision can combine to make him—this, seeker, is the promise of America."[52]

GREAT FOUNDATIONS

In the early 1940s there were less than 1,000 in-dependent foundations. Now, some five decades later, *The Foundation Directory* reckons there to be more than 42,000 active grant making foundations in the United States.[53]

The evolution of the independent foundation in the United States is an interesting study of the application of twentieth-century corporate and management principles to the giving of personal wealth by business leaders and moneyed families. As foundations have grown more and more influential in decisions, combining and augmenting the resources and energy from the public and private sectors, a so-called "independent sector" has been created.[54]

The "sector" concept can be stated simply as follows: there are three controlling sectors in our post-industrial society, originating the initiatives and making the critical decisions that determine the course of Americans' lives and shape their destinies. They are the public sector, (essentially the government); the private sector (businesses, corporations, and other for-profit activity); and the independent sector (which brings together resources from each of the other two sectors to help effect societal change).

David Rockefeller has made statements that have clarified and sorted out this process and its consequences in this way:

- Corporations must develop more effective tools for measuring the social, as well as the economic, costs and benefits of their actions.
- Businessmen must take the initiative to spell out more clearly and positively the longer-range economic and technical implications of current proposals for social problem-solving.
- (We must) assess what business can and cannot do to meet social goals [and] set strategies to combine the strength of public and private resources.
- Strengthen our general understanding of who is responsible for what.[55]

An admirable goal, that, and it can be stated without contradiction, that the Coca-Cola-related foundations are at the very cutting edge of this process by supplying strength and expertise at each step of the process. In doing so, these foundations are adding a completely additional—and desirable—dimension to the philanthropy created by their founding donors.

Indeed, few of the independent foundations in America have outdone those chartered with the wealth created by the Coca-Cola business. The great leaders who gave these entities life are perpetuated in twenty-one representative foundations. Nineteen had their genesis in Georgia, two in Tennessee. Their combined assets amount to over $8 billion. Several of the twenty-one are managed from a single office in Atlanta's Hurt Building. They include the Robert W. Woodruff Foundation, the Lettie Pate Evans and the Lettie Pate Whitehead Foundations, and the Joseph B. Whitehead Foundation. Upon entering the foundations' anteroom, it is no surprise that portraits of these three individuals dominate the space.[56]

Lettie Pate Evans Whitehead was the first female to serve on the board of The Coca-Cola Company, her tenure lasting over two decades. One of her principal advisors in business affairs after the death of her husband was none other than Robert Woodruff, and it is he who saw to her appointment on the Coke board. The total of Lettie Pate Evans Whitehead funds and foundations now approximate those of the Woodruff.[57]

In Chattanooga, George Hunter (heir of Benjamin Thomas) and Cartter Lupton, son of J. T. Lupton, contributed mightily with their foundations, Benwood and Lyndhurst, respectively.[58] The fruit of their labors, combined with their civic leadership and enterprise to reclaim their city, is described in chapter two.

In Columbus, patriarch W. C. Bradley, son-in-law D. Abbott Turner, grandson William B. Turner, and other family members created a foundation intent on producing a like miracle for Columbus. "The Columbus Challenge" is the catalyst in that effort designed to stimulate an extraordinary degree of participation among all sectors of influence and leadership in the city along the mighty Chattahoochee River.[59]

Foundations formed by four Coca-Cola bottler family dynasties are also working to transform their former Georgia territories: the Montgomerys, Cobbs, Haleys, and Samses. Another source of philanthropy has been the Columbus Roberts family of Columbus. Roberts made a remarkable 1937 bequest to Mercer University of $1 million (an amount that today approximates $22 million.) The Barron family, as well, has contributed mightily to the upbuilding of the cities and educational institutions in their old territory.[60]

All of these Coca-Cola-related donors have directed their philanthropy toward causes, institutions, and initiatives in harmony with the heartbeats of their respective "territories" and customers. That, after all, was consonant with the noblest impulses and fondest desires of "your friendly neighbor who bottles Coca-Cola."

"A man of enormous stature and personal magnetism, Robert W. Woodruff's influence over the affairs of The Coca-Cola Company was absolute until his death in 1985," states a printed document describing the history, program, and administration of The Robert W. Woodruff Foundation. There is nothing overstated in that assessment, although some would insist that Woodruff's influence extended far beyond The Coca-Cola Company itself.[61]

The foundation's "broad charter to support charitable, scientific and education activities" permits it to make grants to nonprofit organizations in Georgia. Its principal giving interests are in education, health care, youth services, economic development and civic affairs, art and cultural activities, and the environment. As of the end of 1997, the foundation's assets totaled about $3.7 billion. It is among the ten largest foundations in the nation, ranking above the Carnegie and the Rockefeller.[62]

The Woodruff Foundation has been the subject of considerable attention from news media, especially as the value of the foundation's holdings in Coca-Cola Company stock soared. The attention likely would not have been all that welcome in the early days of its operation, owing to Woodruff's desire to remain anonymous. However, it is not possible to maintain anonymity indefinitely, say some knowledgeable of foundations' ways of the world.[63]

Says Pete McTier, the Woodruff Foundation's president, "for a long time in Atlanta, when a major gift was made and attributed to the 'anonymous donor,' people assumed that the individual had to be Mr. Woodruff. Or they might just dismiss it with, 'Oh, that's the Coca-Cola money.'" But he adds, that was not always the case, citing an instance when the donor was another largely anonymous local source. "It's true," McTier adds, that "so much civic investment in Atlanta arose from the success of Coca-Cola. [But] Mr. Woodruff always was modest in his style of giving even as he donated large amounts in life."[64]

McTier emphasizes the tremendous contribution to philanthropy made by the Whitehead and related foundations, whose role was often less apparent than that of the Woodruff. However, a page one *Wall Street Journal* story on 20 October 1997, gave full acknowledgment to the roles these foundations have played, and how they have contributed to the uplift of *all* of Georgia and the Southeast.[65]

But despite their origins with the company, "neither the Woodruff nor the Whitehead or Evans foundations construct their gifts around Coca-Cola." That clarification made, McTier is not without knowledge of the Coca-Cola business at the grassroots. He served at one time or another on the boards of bottling operations in New Orleans, Atlanta, and Dallas; as well as in Baton Rouge, Louisiana; Jackson, Mississippi; and Macon and Savannah, Georgia.[66]

Pete McTier speaks of the need to "broaden the picture" of the Coca-Cola business and explain the totality of its many diverse elements, especially as it regards philanthropy and the history of the sources of the underlying wealth. It is equally important, he says, "to lift up these families and the enterprises they started with 'Coca-Cola money,'" and to "define their leadership roles in the community." This book attempts to accomplish just that, by trying to chart the "gross philanthropic product" of a number of leading families and individuals in the Coca-Cola business through the years.[67]

During his final days, Coca-Cola Company CEO Roberto Goizueta joined forces with W. B. (Bill) Turner – grandson of W. C. Bradley and son of D. Abbott Turner. All three had been persons of historic dimensions in the Coca-Cola business. A suggestion was made, probably at the behest of Turner, and seconded by Goizueta. "Let's call all the foundations together and share our vision of the future; after, all we're the same kind of people, and we can learn from one another." It is in such instances when the respective directions of these foundations are studied together that one can properly assess the cumulative effect of the philanthropy. The "tale of the tape" – the numbers as to assets and grants – is only one measure; strong, viable communities are another.[68]

What seems evident is how the contributions of these foundations, and the underlying sources of wealth coming from the Coca-Cola business, changed the face of the American South – and perhaps even its heart.

Present in these donors' inspirations were the spiritual influences upon them and the earnest belief in enlightened philanthropy as a means to build up the less fortunate. Two present-day Georgia clerics—Bishop Bevel Jones of the Methodist Church and Dr. J. Davison Philips, former president of Presbyterian-connected Columbia Seminary— speak knowledgeably of the connection between faith and contributions of people such as Lettie Pate Whitehead Evans, J. Bulow Campbell, George Hunter, Asa G. Candler, Robert W. Woodruff, and the Lupton and Bradley families.

From conversation with Jones and Philips, one can gain an insight into the meaning of Andrew Carnegie's essay, "The Gospel of Wealth," or the long-term impact of Rev. J. Russell Conwell's acclaimed message, "Acres of Diamonds." There indeed is a linkage between the donors' faith, their character, and their philanthropy. And they had a remarkable clarity of purpose when it came to the potential impact on their communities.[69]

Conwell's tremendously influential sermon, "Acres of Diamonds," was repeated endlessly before religious audiences and at such events as the Chautauquas. The parable told of an African tribesman who, upon learning of the precious gems, set out on a long journey to find them and make his fortune. Returning to his home years later, he found that the largest diamond mines in the world lay underneath the very land he formerly had occupied. The Coca-Cola-related donors may have taken to heart the passage Conwell emphasized wherever he went:

Any man may be great, but the best place to be great is at home. They can make their kind better; they can labor to help their neighbors and instruct and improve the minds of men, women and children around them....(T)hey can build up the schools and churches around them....These are the elements of greatness, it is here greatness begins, and if a man is not great in his own hometown or in his own school district he will never be great anywhere.[70]

Carnegie, at this same time, was of like mind on "The Gospel of Wealth." He had a credo similar to that of Conwell and one remarkably consonant with those of the foundation donors written of here. Carnegie would write in his timely essay:

> This, then, is held to be the duty of the man of wealth: To set an example of modest, unostentatious living, shunning display or extravagance; to provide moderately for the legitimate wants of those dependent upon him; and after doing so, to consider all surplus revenues which come to him simply as trust funds, which he is called upon to administer in the manner in which, in his judgment, is best calculated to produce the most beneficial results for the community....[71]

Moving from these injunctions, Methodist Bishop Bevel Jones sheds light on the philanthropy of Candler, Whitehead, and Woodruff. Candler was grounded in "faith-in-action," which had deep roots in the Wesleyan tradition of Methodism. The source the bishop finds so powerful is made most evident in the book, *Asa G. Candler*, written by Asa's son, Charles Howard Candler. Several of the son's observations follow:

> His ambition for success and his keen competitive instinct led him to take pleasure in the conduct of his business affairs, it is true. But at no time was the

accumulation of wealth an end in itself to him. He had a profound reverence for his creator, an abiding faith in the revealed word, a complete reliance on the Blood of the Cross, and an unbounded love for his fellow man. For more than half a century, he was a Sunday School teacher or Sunday School superintendent.[72]

It was Candler's firm conviction that religion in the soul "raises the productive force of any life to its highest power. It quickens intellectual facilities, arouses industry, and inspires inventiveness." Moreover, he arrived at a central tenet to his faith, which was this: "The family, the school, and the pulpit are the three main agencies for the conversion of the world. No one of these agencies can be safely ignored or neglected by the church, nor can any one of them operate to the best advantage without the cooperation of the other two."[73]

About the time Candler made these statements, Andrew Carnegie offered $1 million in support of Emory College, provided that the existing board of trustees—run in essence by the Candlers—would be replaced and that the institution be totally free of the influence of "any sect," be it "a Methodist Conference or Presbyterian Assembly or a Catholic order." In response, Asa Candler took a stand, saying, "Education, to be socially useful, and if it is to accomplish the highest results in the creation of personal character, must be penetrated through and through...with moral purpose and religious life." Candler then matched the Carnegie offer—and eventually exceeded it several times over—moving Emory College from Oxford, Georgia, and helping transform it into a prestigious and comprehensive Methodist University in the Druid Hills section of Atlanta.[74]

Dr. Davison Philips is quite knowledgeable about the tremendous influence Presbyterian leaders have had on Coca-Cola-related philanthropy. He cites the roles played by the likes of J. Bulow Campbell and John T. Lupton (with the latter, especially in regards to Oglethorpe University). He notes that the "stock has been very important to the endowments of institutions like Columbia Theological Seminary" and points out that when the Presbyterian seminary faced closing or possibly a merger into Union Seminary, it was Campbell who arranged to have the school moved its present site in Decatur, Georgia. Agnes Scott College, with its deep roots in the denomination, is another institution that benefitted from Campbell's philanthropy, as has Berry College in Rome.[75]

Davison Philips notes a tribute to Campbell by John A. Sibley when dedicating the John Bulow Campbell Science Hall at Agnes Scott in 1951. The wise and far-seeing Sibley spoke volumes in a few words about Campbell—and, by extension, other Coca-Cola related donors—when he said:

In his Last Will and Testament he made a solemn declaration [creating a trust and a foundation], 'There is nothing more worthwhile or of more lasting benefit to humanity than the development and preservation of a love of Jesus Christ.' Through his life and through the foundation that he created, the development of an entire section of the country has been advanced.

The arm of the church has been made more far reaching; the standards of education have been improved in our institutions; the suffering of the weak and helpless has been relieved; the processes that make for new wealth have been stimulated; all those things will continue for years to come and I hope in perpetuity.[76]

Particularly relevant in any assessment of Campbell and his ilk, according to Philips, is the dictum of John Sibley's that is contained in the same remarks cited earlier: "He knew the interdependence of the material, human, and spiritual values. And he knew to achieve stability and permanence, material values must be sustained and supported by human and spiritual values. Upon the foundation of such qualities his success in life was built."[77]

The values of the great majority of Coca-Cola bottlers were much the same as those of John Bulow Campbell. Affirming that many of the pioneering bottlers rose from humble beginnings, an annual report of Chattanooga's Benwood Foundation "called the roll" of several outstanding Thomas Company bottlers who accomplished singular things in the worlds of both bottling and philanthropy. These bottlers are held up as heroes in the Horatio Alger mold—hard-working, honest, thrifty. Among them, Jim Crass, who had built Chattanooga's Incline Railway; Arthur Pratt, a shoe salesman from Alabama, who established bottling enterprises in New York and New Jersey; "Uncle Jim" Pidgeon, a bartender who "set many standards of industry excellence;" Luther Carson, another pioneer who left his job as a railroad conductor; and Crawford Johnson, the former produce salesman and assistant clerk of county court, who brought to life a multistate bottling empire run out of Birmingham, Alabama.[78]

These Thomas Company entrepreneurs' achievements were matched by those of the six great families in Georgia—the Roberts, Cobb, Haley, Montgomery, Barron, and Sams families. Their legacies remain in their hometowns and Main Streets.

The reader will come to his or her own conclusion as to the character, intelligence, and social consciousness of those in the Coca-Cola business profiled here. I submit that the record I examined — and the individuals I interviewed and/or once worked beside — yielded nothing that would cause me to belittle either the bottlers, the company personnel, or their social and civic virtue. True, like J. Bulow Campbell, they found new ways to stimulate wealth. But they also, like Campbell, "knew the interdependence of material, human and spiritual values."[79] And, largely because of their unique contributions, an entire state and an entire region was upbuilt and uplifted.

Endnotes

[1] The Coca-Cola Company Archives, Atlanta, Georgia.

[2] Thurman Sensing, "Sensing the News," newspaper columns for Southern States Industrial Council, Memphis, Tennessee. See also Thurman Sensing, *Down South* (Nashville TN: Southern States Industrial Council, 1945); Emergency Council, *Economic Conditions of the South*, prepared for the President, 22 June 1938, 5-8; Southern Regional Education Board, *Education and Progress in the South, 1938-1998* (Atlanta: Southern Regional Education Board, 1998) 3-15; Doug Cumming, "South's Rise Again Shown after 60 Years," *Atlanta Journal-Constitution*, 18 June 1998, D3-15.

[3] *1997 Annual Report* (Atlanta: The Coca-Cola Company, 1998), share-owners letter from M. Douglas Ivester, chairman and chief executive officer, 3-8. See also Ram Charan, "Managing to be Best: The Century's Smartest Bosses Have Influence Beyond Their Companies," *Time*, 7 December 1998, 107, 127. The *Time* article lists Goizueta as being not only among the 100 titans of twentieth-century commerce, but cites him as one of four exemplary professionals.

[4] Frank Callan Norris, *At Last to Kiss Amanda* (New York: McGraw-Hill, 1961) 35-36.

[5] Charan, "Managing to be Best."

[6] Hirsch was accorded great respect by the bottlers inasmuch as he, too, was one. See Norris, *At Last to Kiss Amanda*; W. C. Bradley Company Archives, Columbus, Georgia; The Coca-Cola Company Archives.

[7] Frederick Allen, *Secret Formula: How Brilliant Marketing and Relentless Salesmanship Made Coca-Cola the Best-Known Product in the World* (New York: Harper Business, 1994); Joseph W. Jones, conversation with author, Atlanta, Georgia, circa 1960.

[8] W. C. Bradley Company Archives.

[9] Ibid.; William B. Turner, W. C. Bradley Company, interview by author, Columbus, Georgia, 27 January 1998.

[10] Columbus Bank and Trust is an integral part of what has become Synovus Financial Corporation, a $9 billion dollar entity that

operates thirty-six banks throughout the South and owns more than eighty percent of Total System Services, Inc. That entity is one of the world's largest credit, debit, commercial, and private-label card processing companies. See "W. C. Bradley Dies...Rites Today," *Columbus Ledger-Enquirer*, 27 July 1947, 1; W. B. Turner, interview by author, Columbus, Georgia, 27 January 1947; Etta Blanchard Worsley, *Columbus on the Chattahoochee* (Columbus GA: Columbus Office Supply, 1951); Pam Baker, "New Face of Columbus Emerging," *Georgia Trend*, June 1998, 50-51.

[11] "W C. Bradley Dies...Rites Today," 1; W. C. Bradley Company Archives; Susan Wiggins, W. C. Bradley Company, interview by author, Columbus, Georgia, 27 January 1998.

[12] John Koenig, "Columbus: A City that Has Preserved its Rich Heritage," *Athens Daily News and Athens Banner-Herald*, 8 December 1996, C11; W C. Bradley Company Archives; Baker, "New Face of Columbus Emerging," 54-55.

[13] Wiggins interview; "W C. Bradley Dies...Rites Today," 1; Board resolution from Columbus Bank & Trust Co. in praise of D. Abbott Turner, W. C. Bradley Company Archives.

[14] W. C. Bradley Company Archives; *The Foundation Directory* (New York: The Foundation Center, 1998).

[15] James M Blanchard, letter to the author, 17 April 1998. Once named Georgia's CEO of the year by *Georgia Trend*, Blanchard's issue of Synovus was cited in the 11 January 1999 issue of *Fortune* as the top employer in the nation for which to work.

[16] Ibid.

[17] Baker, "New Face of Columbus Emerging," 49.

[18] Ibid.

[19] Ibid.

[20] Robert W. Woodruff, letter to W. C. Bradley, 5 February 1935, Robert W. Woodruff Collection, Emory University Library, Atlanta, Georgia.

[21] Latimer Watson, "Big Coke Controversy is Raging Undiminished," *Columbus Ledger-Enquirer*, 12 February 1960, 8.

[22] Ibid.

[23] Inscription on State Capitol of California, Sacramento, as quoted in speech by Arch N. Booth, executive vice president, Chamber of Commerce of the United States, circa 1959.

[24] Ivan Allen Jr., interview by author, Atlanta, Georgia, 17 March 1998.

[25] Ibid.

[26] Ibid.; Harrison Jones II, interview by author, Atlanta, Georgia, 23 January 1998.

[27] W. Frank Barron, interview by author, Rome, Georgia, 18 April 1998.

[28] Ralph McGill, "Coca-Cola's 'Engine': Harrison Jones Plans Retirement," *Atlanta Constitution*, 1 June 1952, 11; James Saxon Childers, "Harrison Jones...He Has Helped Make Atlanta Great," *Atlanta Journal and Constitution Magazine*, 1 July 1956; *Westminster School Alumni News*, Summer-Fall 1994, 28-30.

[29] *Westminster School Alumni News*.

[30] Thomas W. Reed, *David Crenshaw Barrow* (Athens GA: Self-published, 1935) 35-36.

[31] Arthur L. Montgomery, interview by author, Atlanta, Georgia, 11 October 1998; James W. Wimberly, interview by author, Atlanta, Georgia, 17 September 1998.

[32] McGill, "Coca-Cola's 'Engine': Harrison Jones Plans Retirement," 11.

[33] Sanders Rowland, interview by author, Asheville, North Carolina, 24 December 1988.

[34] Wimberly interview; Keats Dunnam Jr., Corpus Christi Coca-Cola Bottling Company, conversation with the author, Corpus Christi, Texas, circa 1963; Ovid R. Davis, conversation with the author, Atlanta, Georgia, circa 1960.

[35] Harrison Jones, "Our Heritage and Our Future," speech to bottlers, 1948, collection of Harrison Jones II.

[36] J. Paul Austin, recollection of the author; "Chautauqua Movement," *The New Encyclopedia Britannica*, (Chicago: Encyclopedia Britannica, Inc., 1985) 3:142.

[37] Internal memorandum, The Coca-Cola Company Archives.

[38] Jones's evangelical fervor served the enterprise well. Onetime chairman H. Burke Nicholson, in fact, took care not to let this quality

absent the scene where the business was concerned. He sounded a call just before Jones's retirement for others like the man to come forward. Nicholson wrote: "The flag bearers, holders-up of the torch, seekers of the Holy Grail, even the Don Quixotes jousting with windmills, do not seem to be present as of old. Where is the leadership that formerly made people in this institution feel that they belong to a Church to which they gave unquestioned obedience, loyalty and fidelity? Some strong characters must lift up the flag else this Thing recedes into the limbo of just another corporation, just another organized group, and not some great warm moving purposeful crusade." Jones II interview. See also *The Red Barrel*, April 1936, 8-9; it contains examples of state-of-the-art (for its day) motivational communication and examples of industrial theater.

[39] William T. Campbell, *The Big Beverage* (Kingsport TN: Kingsport Press, 1952) 35-37; Jones, "Our Heritage and Our Future."

Said Jones, "It's only when you have more than one dollar, it's only when you get up in the world — when you've lost your calluses off your hand, when you don't have to bathe every day on account of the sweat; when you've forgotten the smell of the earth that you have an argument. Your forebears in the early days did not get beyond that crude description."

[40] "Coca-Cola Pioneer Rainwater Dies," *Atlanta Journal*, 24 April 1973. Company president J. Lucian Smith sent a letter to all bottlers announcing the veteran Coke man's death and praising his achievements.

See also Lillian Hooper Hardison, "Coca-Cola Bottling Plants in Georgia: The Preservation of Standardized Early 20th Century Commercial Buildings" (master's thesis, University of Georgia, 1994) 34-36. Hardison's work represents a significant contribution to the accumulated lore concerning Rainwater's Standardization Committee and its greatest feat — effectively gaining agreement on key issues affecting the business from some twelve hundred constituencies, the body of bottlers, as well as The Coca-Cola Company and its vendors.

[41] The Coca-Cola Company Archives; *The Red Barrel*.

[42] News release, The Coca-Cola Company, 4 April 1973.

[43] Correspondence of Harold Hirsch related to the university and athletic scholarships, University of Georgia Athletic Association Archives, Athens, Georgia; printed program, Dedicatory Exercises of Harold Hirsch Hall and Alexander Campbell King Memorial Library, University of Georgia School of Law, Athens, Georgia, 1932, Robert W. Woodruff Collection, Emory University.

[44] Kilpatrick & Stockton Archives (successor firm of Candler, Thomson, and Hirsch), Atlanta, Georgia, as provided by Miles J. Alexander, partner.

[45] Ibid.; Della Wages Wells, *The First Hundred Years: A Centennial History of King & Spalding* (Atlanta: King & Spalding, 1985) 137-164. Interestingly enough, it was the Spalding-Sibley combine that weighed in on behalf of the franchisees in those early jousts. In fact, there is some evidence that Hirsch made it possible for this duo to end up representing the company, while Hirsch and his firm—including Marion Smith and M. E. "Buster" Kilpatrick—began to represent the bottlers. But as those who know the business well know, there is ample evidence of the absolutely dominant role the law and lawyers have played in the affairs of the Coca-Cola System. And the major players in that regard have been Hirsch, Sibley, and Spalding— although others have played prominent parts, as well. One such was Pope F. Brock. After Harrison Jones stepped down as chairman at The Coca-Cola Company, Jones brought Brock over to join him at Fulton National Bank, making Brock chairman.

[46] Even the dedication's musical prelude and postlude were furnished by the first cousin of Mrs. Robert Woodruff, Hugh Hodgson, professor of music at the university. (Years later the Robert W. Woodruff Foundation made a multimillion dollar grant to the University of Georgia to help build Hugh Hodgson Hall at its performing arts center.) And perhaps out of deference to Hirsch, the benediction was pronounced by a clergyman identified only as Rabbi Schusterman. See Hirsch Hall dedication program.

[47] Hirsch Hall dedication program.

[48] Sinclair, Townes & Company's Foundation Directory and Service for Georgia (1998), Foundation Center, Atlanta, Georgia.

[49] Dan Magill, "Roddenbery to Receive Bill Hartman Award," *Athens Daily News and Athens Banner-Herald*, 19 November 1998, C1.

[50] Lyons Joel, "A Legal Giant and a Great Humanitarian," *The Jewish Georgian*, July-August 1997, 1.

[51] *Georgia Alumni Record*, "In Memoriam—Harold Hirsch," Fall 1939, 7.

[52] Roddenbery's den in his Hamilton home houses mementos related to his medical career and to his athletic coaches and teammates. It also features framed photographs of his benefactors with The Coca-Cola Company—Jones and Hirsch.

See S. A. Roddenbery, *I Swear by Apollo* (Hamilton GA: Grandy Press, 1994); "Roddenbery Receives Hartman Award," news release, University of Georgia Sports Communications, 20 November 1998. Also, S. Anderson Roddenbery, M.D., interview by author, Hamilton, Georgia, 25 January 1998.

The story of Delmar Edwards, the surgeon, is a moving one recounted in the monograph of Benjamin F. Pike, M.D., "Living Convictions: The Early Life of Andy Roddenbery," Columbus, Georgia, February 1998. See also Thomas Wolfe, *You Can't Go Home Again* (New York: Harper & Brothers, 1940) 636.

[53] *Foundation Directory*.

[54] Ibid; Brian O'Connell, *Powered by Coalition: The Story of the Independent Sector* (San Francisco: Jossey-Bass, 1997), foreword by John William Gardner, ix-xii. The Rockefellers, David and John D., have used slightly different terminology in describing that sector of society apart from the public (government) and private (enterprise), designating that sector as "the third sector."

[55] David Rockefeller, *Vital Speeches*, 1 April 1977, 43: 357-360.

[56] *Foundation Directory*; Sinclair, Townes service; Charles H. McTier, interviews by author, Atlanta, Georgia, 9 June 1998, and 10 November 1998; brochure, The Robert W. Woodruff Foundation; brochure, The Whitehead Foundation. See also "The Philanthropic Legacy of Coca-Cola," *Chronicle of Philanthropy*, 19 September 1996, 12.

[57] McTier interview.

[58] The Benwood Foundation annual report for 1995 credits the example of Robert Woodruff's foundation as the inspiration for the founding of Benwood in 1945. See *1995 Annual Report* (Chattanooga TN: The Benwood Foundation, 1996); *1997 Annual Report*

(Chattanooga TN: Lyndhurst Foundation, 1998). The latter features a message from the foundation's president, Jack Murrah, in which he discusses the remarkable results of a multi-sector coalition seeking to bring about social renewal and economic revival to the area. See also Melissa Turner, "Pardon Me, Boys, is THIS Chattanooga?" *Atlanta Journal-Constitution*, 20 April 1998, E1.

[59] "Area Focus: Columbus," *Georgia Trend*, June 1998.

[60] Spright Dowell, *Columbus Roberts: Christian Steward Extraordinary* (Nashville TN: Broadman Press, 1951); R Kirby Godsey, letter to the author, 11 August 1997, 1.

[61] A pair of entries chronicle some of the many ways in Woodruff quietly wielded power. They are: Sam Heys, "Woodruff Helped Make Atlanta What it Is Today,"*Atlanta Journal-Constitution*, 7 May 1986, H2; Harold Martin, *This Happy Isle* (Sea Island GA: Sea Island Company, 1978) 138-139, 162-165.

[62] Woodruff Foundation brochure; *Foundation Directory*.

[63] McTier interview.

[64]Ibid. The foundation president notes that changed circumstances have altered the anonymity guideline for specific source of bequests.

[65] Nikhil Deogun, "The Legacy: Roberto Goizueta Led Coca-Cola Stock Surge, and Its Home Prospers," *Wall Street Journal*, 20 October 1997, A1.

[66] McTier interview.

[67] Ibid.

[68] W. B. Turner, interview by author, Columbus, Georgia, 27 January 1998; Gary Pomerantz, "Atlanta's Growth Stock," *Atlanta Journal-Constitution*, 27 October 1995, H7.

[69] Andrew Carnegie, *The Gospel of Wealth* (Cambridge MA: Harvard University Press, 1962) 25, 52, 821-831. See also J. Russell Conwell, *Acres of Diamonds* (Philadelphia: J. B. Lippincott, 1887) 99-100.

[70] Conwell, *Acres of Diamonds*.

[71] Carnegie, *The Gospel of Wealth*, 25, 52, 821-831.

[72] Charles Howard Candler, *Asa G. Candler* (Atlanta: Emory University, 1950). A biography written by the son of Asa G. Candler, chapter 10 of this book deals with the elder Candler's dedication to

education, and Emory University; Christian philanthropy, 337-351; and Candler's public service, 327-335.

73 Ibid.

74 Ibid. One only has to look to the fruit of Candler's faith in action to know this is no pietistic posturing. Among his beneficiaries are Emory University and Emory Medical School, Wesley Memorial Church and Wesley Memorial Enterprises, and Emory University Hospital. But the philanthropist also discovered a useful device for compounding his considerable contributions. That was the offering of gifts conditioned upon a church's, an electorate's, or an educational institution's matching the gift. Since Candler's instituting the practice—at "Ingathering Day" for the hospital on Christmas Day 1904, for Atlanta Methodists—virtually all of the twenty-one foundations studied have utilized the matching gifts idea to great advantage for their communities or constituencies. The practice was jointly conceived by Asa G. Candler and his brother, Methodist Bishop Warren A. Candler. And both of the brothers, not so coincidentally, played the key roles in the creation of what is now Emory University, with Asa serving as president of the board of trustees of Emory University—the now-moved-to-Atlanta school, on land donated by him—from its organization until his death in 1929. Brother Warren was the school's first chancellor.

75 Philips interview.

76 John A. Sibley, address, dedication of John Bulow Campbell Science Hall, Agnes Scott College, 31 October 1951. For a detailed biography of Campbell, see Lucian Lamar Knight, *A Standard History of Georgia and Georgians, volume VI* (Chicago and New York: Lewis Publishing Co., 1917) 3002-3003.

77 Ibid.

78 Benwood Foundation, *1995 Annual Report,* 9.

79 Sibley address.

INDEX